YOU'LL WIN NOTHING
WITH KIDS

Also by Jim White

Are You Watching, Liverpool?
The Diary of Darren Tackle

YOU'LL WIN NOTHING WITH KIDS

Fathers, Sons and Football

Jim White

Little, Brown

LITTLE, BROWN

First published in Great Britain in 2007 by Little, Brown
Reprinted 2007 (five times)

A CIP catalogue record for this book
is available from the British Library.

ISBN 978-0-316-02982-7

Typeset in Bembo by Palimpsest Book Production Limited,
Grangemouth, Stirlingshire
Printed and bound in Great Britain by Clays Ltd, St Ives plc

Little, Brown
An imprint of
Little, Brown Book Group
100 Victoria Embankment
London EC4Y 0DY

An Hachette Livre UK Company

www.littlebrown.co.uk

To the lads

Contents

Introduction

Who is that prat?

Just look at him, the touchline wally. What kind of figure does he think he is cutting, with his shouty red face and his jabby finger? There he is, overheated and overexcited, as if what is going on is the final of the Champions League, not a fixture in the local youth football league, under-14 section. Can he not see that he is a comedy staple? Does he not realise that he is a stereotype of our times: the stressed-out manager of a boys' football team? He seems to think it is appropriate on a Sunday morning to stalk the side of a pitch while a few kids kick a ball around, behaving as if he is Alex Ferguson patrolling the Old Trafford technical area. Now he's off again, throwing his arms over his head in dismay at a missed chance, making a wild windmilling gesture with his right arm, shouting something only marginally coherent at the players that might be 'Coomon lads' or 'You can do it.'

Oh dear, look at him now. The opposition have just scored and he has turned his back on the pitch. His head is down, he is kicking at the ground, a little puff of dust rising in front of him every time he scuffs the turf with the sole of his shoe. He really is a sad, sorry sight. Someone should take a video of him. It would be a useful tool in FA training sessions: how not to retain your touchline composure. At the very least, I should snap him on my phone, just as an aide-memoire of how you really shouldn't behave in these circumstances.

There is, however, just one problem with such an idea. I am that touchline wally. I am that unhinged fool. I am that prat. And the fact is, even if I could take a snap of myself, my phone is in no fit state for photography, as I have just taken it out of my pocket and flung it to the ground, together with my car keys and about £1.48 in loose change. Even as I behave like this, even as I watch the phone cartwheel away across the grass, its battery separating from the back and heading off in the direction of the ring road, I know how ridiculous I must look. I think of Sven-Göran Eriksson, for five years as England head coach exhibiting a dug-out demeanour of calm and detachment, somehow managing, in the midst of turmoil, to maintain the emotional poise of a bag of frozen peas. Yet he was responsible for a team in which was invested the expectations of tens of millions of people. What he did mattered; how his team performed had real resonance, a nation's well-being depended on whether or not he extracted a satisfactory performance from his players. Me, my only responsibility is for the feelings of sixteen adolescents, their parents, step-parents and the odd same-sex life partner. But somehow I can't help myself. Right now, if you wired my blood pressure up to the national grid, you could run a small conurbation for a week.

As it happens, this scene does not represent a high point in my coaching life. It is the last game of the football season and the team I am in charge of, Northmeadow

Youth, are involved in a relegation struggle of such dimensions, with so many possible outcomes, that had a tabloid sports reporter been assigned to cover the match, the only word he could find adequately to describe its scale would be 'titanic'. This morning, depending on results, five teams could go down. And there are only ten in the whole league. Our position is simpler than that of some of our rivals: win and we stay up. Any other result and we are down, no matter what happens elsewhere.

Right now, though, our survival chances have just been hit square-on by an iceberg. We are holed below the waterline. Worse, the band has stopped playing, is about to be washed overboard by a freak wave and none of the rhythm section knows how to swim.

This most vital of games is approaching half-time and we have just conceded another goal. The score now stands at 3-0. Our opponents, who also need to win to remain in the elite, are currently celebrating their latest success over by the corner flag. The boy who scored with a free-kick of such precision and poise David Beckham would be pushed to match it, is performing a pre-rehearsed routine involving the imaginary spinning of discs on a DJ's turntable. It is one he might well have seen on television and which he has clearly spent some time choreographing in preparation for this moment. He has one hand cupped to his ear as if he is holding a set of headphones, while with the other he is making circling gestures as if scratching a record. His colleagues gather round him, jiggling their shoulders and making hip hop-inspired finger movements; they look like Edward Scissorhands without the scissors. On the far touchline, our rival supporters are in the middle of a quickstep of delight, the beam of their smiles flashing across the pitch. On our side, the parents, step-parents and the odd same-sex life partner stand in silence, frozen in their despair.

It seems that unless fortune changes with an improbability not even Hollywood scriptwriters would dare suggest, we will be playing in the second division next season, a swift and unplanned-for retreat just one year on from promotion. This, then, is when a coach comes into his own. With the referee about to blow for half-time, this is the moment when clear-headed instructions and precisely delivered tactical analysis could make all the difference. By turning round the holed ship with a few well-chosen words, this could be his chance, his opportunity to do something other than implode in impotent frustration. This is when all the greats earn their crust. José Mourinho, Rafa Benitez, Arsène Wenger, Fergie himself: what they would say in these circumstances would make all the difference.

Before I can do any of that, though, before I can match their rhetoric, before I can effect a rescue plan, before I can dredge the appropriate rallying call from the depths of my memory, I have to scan the turf for the bits of my phone. And when I've found them, piece them together and see if it still works.

'This what you're looking for?' asks one of the opposition supporters, a large bloke who has been standing on our side of the pitch throughout the first half, encouraging his grandson in a rumbling Welsh baritone ('Get stuck in, Rhys'). He is now holding up my battery.

'Oh yeah, thanks,' I say. 'Look, I'm really sorry about . . .' I gesture back at the touchline, now restored to a civilised calm, 'you know . . . all that.'

'Don't worry, mate, think nothing of it,' he says, kindly. 'That's boys' football for you.'

★　　★　　★

I thought about that comment for ages afterwards. He was right: that is boys' football for you. In my job as a sports reporter, I've seen a few events. In the Camp Nou in May 1999, the noise that came from my mouth when Ole Gunnar Solskjær scored the winner for Manchester United in the Champions League final sounded rather like a dog getting its tail jammed in a car door. At the Oval in September 2005, I greeted the umpires' signal for bad light that meant the Ashes had finally returned to England after eighteen years Down Under with an explosion of profanities. When Kelly Holmes burst past the rest of the field in the Olympic Stadium in Athens in 2004 to win her second gold medal, in the press seats the bloke sitting next to me and I were locked in such a passionate embrace any observer would assume marriage was imminent.

But Olympic Games, FA Cup finals, the Six Nations, the rare occasions when the horse I backed has come home anywhere near the winner's enclosure at Cheltenham, none of them has the resonance of your own flesh and blood hoofing a ball around, or surviving a tight lbw appeal, or emerging intact from the bottom of a muddy ruck. It doesn't matter the level, it doesn't matter the competence, nothing makes you as nervy, as jittery. Nothing fills you with as much pride as their success, nothing makes you suffer like their defeats. Nothing sends you as doolally. Nowhere do you feel as alive.

That is why I am here today. The Sunday-morning phone-calls from your best player crying off with a sniffle; the endless committee meetings with their three-hour debates about whether it is ethically correct to seek sponsorship from a burger company; the push-me-pull-you scuffle in the back of the goal between the fathers of two of your players; the complications of divorced parents squabbling over weekend access to your left winger; the trainee psychopath whose assault on your centre forward's shins is ignored by a myopic referee who turns out to be the assailant's dad; the parent who thinks their son should be the centre forward despite the fact he has yet to master the rudiments of tying his own shoelace; the absolute inability of your right winger to pass the ball to a player wearing the same colour shirt; the way you wake up at three in the morning with a whirr of tactics rushing through your head: none of it can put me off.

I've no idea what it is like for my boy, to try to perform with his father's looming presence blanketing out the touchline sunlight. But I suspect the emotional traffic is almost exclusively one way.

One thing I am certain of is this: I am not alone. About an hour after England's defeat in the 2006 World Cup in Germany, I was walking out of the stadium to catch a bus back into the centre of Gelsenkirchen. All around, a shuffling, shambolic Dunkirk-style retreat was in full flow. The England supporters who had followed their national team for the previous three weeks swathed in such optimism were on their way home, dispirited, defeated, dejected after yet another penalty shoot-out failure in yet another quarter-final. It was still hot enough for unattended small children spontaneously to barbecue on the pavement and all around were necks and thighs and shoulders pinked up by their day in the sun. Banners and colours that had flown with such pride on the way into the stadium were discarded on the way out, trodden into the evening dust. A white and red jester's hat lay in the gutter. Occasionally, a passing fan would kick it and it would roll over. As it did so, its bells would give off a forlorn little tinkle, a sad last post for England's cup.

All around was misery, disappointment and a barely concealed sense that the foot soldiers of the England support had been let down. Let down by the administrators with the feeble inability to secure a sufficient number of tickets to meet demand. Let down by the team management with its emotional sterility, its tactical blunders and its woeful selections. But let down most of all by the players, a bunch which we were repeatedly told, as often by themselves as by anyone else, represented the best in the world, yet had proven to be anything but. These were the playboys of the modern game, earning enough to embarrass an African dictator; spoiled boys with their stables of sports cars, their own-label scents, their spendthrift wives and girlfriends behaving like Marie Antoinette. These were the new upper classes, coveted, cosseted and, as it turned out, crap. Earning £100,000 each and every week and still they couldn't score from twelve yards with only the goalkeeper to beat. The charge against them was a criminal dereliction of duty. And there were few leaving the stadium that evening prepared to argue the players' innocence. In fact, so cheesed off were the supporters, if anyone asked for volunteers to arrest the players, secure the leg irons and chuck away the key, the queue would have stretched halfway home to Blighty.

'Bloody Lampard,' I heard someone say on the way out. 'He should be strung up.'

That was quite mild compared to some responses.

As I waited at the bus stop, however, I became aware of a small group of supporters coming in my direction whose gait made the rest of those leaving look as though they had a spring in their step. This party consisted of a bearded, bandy-legged man, holding on to a small girl's hand. Alongside him were two women, a mother and daughter perhaps. None of them were speaking. Despite the fact they were all well-dressed, tanned, clearly prosperous, they looked so miserable, so defeated, so crestfallen, I couldn't help stare at them. And as I did so, I realised that the man was Frank Lampard Senior, the father of the player targeted for particular blame by the England supporters. He had just watched his son miss a penalty in the shoot-out at the end of a World Cup quarter-final. As it happens, that miss cannot have come as much of a surprise since Frank Junior had spent the whole tournament missing. Twenty-five shots he had in five matches, none of them finding the back of the opponents' net. So prolific a misser was he, his name changed subtly during those three weeks in Germany until he became known as Frank Lampard Surely.

Such gags, though, were not of much use to his dad, walking through the German sunshine, his shoulders sloping at an angle of forty-five degrees, his eyes fixed on the ground, apparently studying the contours of his toes.

'Bad luck, Frank,' I said as the party passed.

He raised his head, nodded lightly and said nothing, nothing at all. But for a second we made eye contact. And at that precise moment, for the first time in the length of the tournament, I felt an empathy with the England team. Suddenly, in one glance, Frank Lampard had changed from being an overrated, overpaid and over-privileged symbol of all that was wrong with English football to being just somebody's lad kicking a ball around. There was something in his father's eyes as he looked back at me, a glancing, momentary revelation. It was a glance that said no one was suffering as much as him.

And that no matter at what level the game was played, no matter how celebrated the participants, no matter how substantial the prize on offer, this is what football is all about: fathers and sons.

Unlike Frank Lampard's, my dad was not a football man. He had absolutely no affection for the game, had never played it in his youth, never watched it in later life. Here's how little he cared about football: when the World Cup was staged in England in 1966, he took the family on a camping holiday in Germany. Mind you, even he was moved to pay attention to that year's final. Though the attention he paid it was somewhat foggy. My only first-hand recollection of English football's finest moment is a seven-year-old's memory of my dad, standing in a camp-site on the banks of the Rhine, with a transistor radio clutched to his ear trying to translate the German coverage for the rest of us. Not that he spoke German.

'Someone called Horst has just scored,' he announced at one point. 'Reckon that means Germany must have won it.'

Even Dad, though, recognised that football had some unspoken part to play in the relationship between father and son. The year I was nine, Manchester United had just won the European Cup and Manchester City the League Championship. The metropolis in which we lived was temporarily the centre of the footballing universe. The finest club team in Europe and the best in England were playing no more than six miles down the road. My dad, showing that unique understanding of the game that he had displayed on the banks of the Rhine, therefore took me off that year to watch Altrincham, then marooned in the amateur Cheshire League. Thus while Law, Best,

Charlton, Lee, Bell and Summerbee were in the ascendant, I became briefly acquainted with the game of Jackie Swindells, the balding, pedestrian, almost perpetually angry Alty centre forward. We would stand on the terracing just opposite the tunnel out of which the players would trot. Here I would subject Dad to the kind of relentless interrogation small boys reserve exclusively for their fathers.

'Dad, why did Jackie Swindells kick that man?'

'Dad, why's the referee pointing?'

'Dad, why is Jackie Swindells walking towards the tunnel?'

'Dad, who is the bastard in the black?'

To which the answers would be: 'I don't know', 'Not sure', 'Who knows' and 'Ask your mother.'

His inability to provide a single adequate response to a single football-related question ('Offside? It's complicated') did not stem the torrent.

'Why do goalkeepers wear green?'

'Good question.'

'Has anyone ever scored from a throw-in?'

'I couldn't tell you.'

'Have United ever bought an Alty player?'

'Ooh, you know, I've never really thought about it.'

It didn't seem to matter to me that my questions weren't answered. Their purpose was not to elicit information. Looking back on them now, I realise it was simply to imitate conversation, to fill the gap between us with something, anything. To take the place of intimacy. But maybe all the questions got to him. After no more than half a dozen visits, those trips to Alty's Moss Lane ground slipped off the weekend agenda. A couple of seasons later, after a brief dalliance with trainspotting, I went to Old Trafford for the first time on my own, to watch Manchester United. And the moment I walked down the Warwick Road, Swindells became ancient history.

As for my own footballing performances, I can count on one finger the number of times Dad must have seen me play a game. Clearly, odd decision-making was in the genes because when I went to grammar school I opted to play lacrosse instead of football. Lacrosse is a game, as I recall it, that involves not much more than being whacked around the knuckles by someone wielding a wooden-framed net as if he had been a gladiator in a former existence. In a damp Mancunian winter, when the hands are raw with cold, it seemed a particularly unnecessary game. I would spend matches cowering from the small, hard ball flung at my head and the sticks seeking out my soft, tender fingers. We once lost 14-0 to a school from Stockport, a match in which my contribution consisted of standing on the wing hoping nobody noticed I was playing. As a tactic, it worked to perfection.

'Were you actually playing out there this afternoon, Chalky?' asked the games master as we trudged back from the school field. 'Only I never noticed.'

Soon after that my association with lacrosse was at an end, its legacy a stick that remained in the umbrella stand in the hall at home until my parents moved about a decade after my last game.

I did play cricket, though. And in the summer Dad was a regular on the boundary. Indeed his loyal presence there was probably responsible for what might laughably be termed the progress of my cricket career.

'Is your dad around Saturday, lad?' Ted, our coach, would often ask after training.

'Yeah, think so,' I'd say.

'Good, then you're in the team. We need another car to get everyone there.'

Dad was a willing chauffeur. And when he got to the match, he was always a discreet spectator. I cannot recall him ever offering loud opinion of the umpire from behind the rope. Nor did he collar Ted after matches to complain about his boy's position in the batting order or ask him why I never got to bowl (perhaps he knew what the answer might be). Nor was he ever critical about my habit of getting out just as double figures approached. 'The nervous nines,' he called it, partly ironically, but mostly sympathetically.

So discreet was he, often I would forget he was there. Which meant I could slip into my default position in the field: the team clown. Arsing about, taking nothing seriously, oozing cynicism about our prospects, that was me. I would do impressions of my team-mates. Mike Bennett, in the slips with his collar up, with his fingers facing the wrong way, dropping an edge was a favourite. Or make fun of their names. Steven Clifford I insisted on calling Rich, right up until the point when, in a whirl of fury, he suddenly lost it and went for me between overs: 'My name is Steve, OK? I am not Rich Clifford.' 'Oooh,' I said, running for the pavilion with him in close pursuit, 'congratulations, Rich. And celebrations.'

Despite Clifford's attempt to remove my head from my shoulders, I carried on playing. And, at the end of the under-14 season, Ted informed me I was on the shortlist for selection for autumn net sessions, run by Lancashire County Cricket Club at Old Trafford. It was, he added, an honour afforded a mere handful of young players locally and if I worked really hard I might get it.

'Sometimes I think buried deep underneath all that

stupid behaviour there could be a cricketer lurking,' he told me. 'But you've a long way to go.'

'Not that far,' I said. 'We only live down the road. And anyway I can get my dad to give me a lift.'

That, now I look back on it, was probably the point that marked the end of my chances of becoming a proper sportsman. Sensing that I had not treated his offer with the seriousness he felt it deserved, in the end Ted gave the place in the nets to Clifford instead. When I told Dad about my near brush with success and how it had been cruelly snatched from me by a Cliff Richard namesake, he just smiled and said, 'Oh well, never mind.'

See, for him sport never really mattered.

The first indication that I was not as my father on the touchline – chilled, relaxed, philosophical, his mind, almost exclusively, elsewhere – came when my eldest son was just six years old. We were living in north London, in a borough renowned for the progressive approach it took on most matters, including education. Here, in the early 1990s, those in charge of educating the next generation had a potent enemy against which they waged daily war: competitiveness. This, for the head teacher at the primary where Hugo had just enrolled, was as pernicious an evil as sexism, racism, in fact any ism at all. It was a spectral remnant from a past of privilege and empire, an insidious presence that needed to be exorcised. Never mind that competition is all the pupils would face when they eventually headed abroad into what the rest of us fondly call the real world; never mind that the spirit of a small child (particularly of the male variety) is driven entirely by the need to compete: within the confines of that school every last vestige of it was frowned upon. Since achievement was a bourgeois notion that undermined the confidence of those lacking the privileges of more supportive backgrounds, at this school there were no prizes for good work. No, everyone shared the praise equally, whether they had achieved anything or not. There were no tests to check if any learning had been done, just to make sure that those who found tests difficult were not prejudiced against. And, above all, there was to be no sport anywhere on the premises. Sport represented competition at its most corrupting: trying to beat someone else at games was, to the mind of the head teacher, morally indefensible. By its very nature, she reckoned, sport discriminated against those who could not perform it. For her, winning was nothing more than a form of abuse and sport a malicious concept that needed to be eradicated.

She and her colleagues had to be vigilant, to suffocate sporting activity whenever it occurred. Like Japanese knotweed, it could appear anywhere at any time, snaring the unwary in a rapidly growing jungle of opposition and rivalry. In the playground, every so often, someone would bring a ball along and the boys would quickly form up a chaotic, twenty-a-side scramble of a game. How the head teacher had to dash from her office to put a stop to that. At the first outbreak of football, she would be out there, confiscating the ball. Though the real reason was to prevent the seeds of competition forming in prepubescent heads, the ban was generally dressed up as a health and safety issue.

'What would happen if you smashed a window? The glass could fly out and take someone's eye out. Have you thought about that?'

Kids, however, are not easily dissuaded. Other forms of competition would quickly spring up to replace the banished ball game. So when the pupils' attention turned to conkers, they had to be banned. Cricket bats were confiscated the moment they appeared in the yard, and when the boys tried instead to play foot cricket, tennis balls were added to the proscribed list. Soon they were joined by marbles, top-trump cards and skipping ropes ('Can you imagine what might happen if someone slipped and fell on to that thing while it's being swung about?').

It was hard work for this modern day Gradgrind, competition could emerge anywhere, at any time. She had to be particularly vigilant come the summer term, when thoughts of parents and children turn to a hardy annual of the school calendar. The first year Hugo was at the school, I innocently asked the head when sports day would be.

'We don't have a sports day,' she said, looking down at me as if I had just asked when the local branch of the KKK were scheduled to hold their annual cross-burning rally. 'At this school we have a non-competitive team activities morning.'

The non-competitive team activities morning took place on one of the few open spaces in the borough. For days before Hugo had been talking about nothing else, daydreaming of breasting the tape in triumph. When I arrived to watch one of my children in sporting action for the first time, it was clear he wasn't the only one excited by the prospect. The place was awash with children's activity. Small people were tearing round all over the place, playing tag, attempting to climb trees, hitting each other with sticks: it was a cheering sight. On one patch of ground, a girl in the top year was stretching and warming up. She looked like Denise Lewis must have done as an eleven-year-old: floaty, graceful, legs like a gazelle. On her feet she had sprinter's spikes, and she was practising her starts, bursting away from imagined blocks with mesmerising athleticism. I thought, I'm looking forward to watching her in the team relay.

Soon, though, the head teacher's bossy tones were wafting across the grass.

'Right, children,' she shouted through a loudhailer she carried with her. 'Let's all form into our teams.'

Each team had been given a name. Not Bulls or Sharks or Lightning, obviously. Not even England, Scotland and Wales. Not even Cuba, Angola and North Korea. No, these were teams named after historical feminist figures: Rosa Parks, Emmeline Pankhurst, Germaine Greer. I asked Hugo what team he was in and he said he thought he was in the wolves. It was Wollstonecraft. Still, he remained full of anticipation as he lined up with his team that mixed older and younger pupils, each looking forward to the fun ahead.

From the first task, though, it was clear this was no sports day as remembered by the parents dotted round the field's edge. There were no dashes or darts, no sprints or scurries. There was nothing three-legged, no hopping, skipping or jumping and definitely no sacks. Instead, in their teams, the children had to undertake a series of ten short relays: ferrying water in small plastic tubes and pouring it into a bucket, say, or putting bricks into colour-coded lines. Running was discouraged ('You might fall over and hurt yourself,' the head teacher explained), so they just had to walk through their event.

Soon the older children were hanging about at the back of their lines looking bored, neither challenged nor stretched. As they stood there, the teachers were cooing about how well everyone was doing.

'Isn't it good to see nobody losing?' I overheard one

teacher say, apparently oblivious to the disappointment and frustration brewing all round.

As things progressed, it became ever more obvious that the non-competitive team challenge was about as popular with the children as an outbreak of mumps. Some would do the tasks with ostentatious ease, their every splosh of water into the bucket a sarcastic gloss on the whole event. Others were deliberately messing things up, putting their legs into the sleeves of blouses in the dressing-up game, or failing to stack the bricks in the build-a-wall relay. Several of the older girls had taken themselves away completely and were sitting under a tree exchanging gossip.

I looked around for the young sprinter and saw she had made her way to the head of her team line, squatting down ready to burst forward to put on a pair of cowboy trousers. I wasn't the only one who had seen her and, before she could launch herself towards her costume, the head teacher asked her what on earth she thought she was doing. The question was picked up by the loudhailer the woman carried and echoed, accusingly, round the field.

'I'm getting down for a start,' the girl said. 'Means you go quicker and that.'

'Well, don't do that, Malika, there's no need to run,' said the head, as if addressing a three-year-old. 'And what on earth have you got on your feet?'

'Running spikes.'

'Well, take them off. We don't use that sort of thing here.'

In other countries, a talent like hers would have been nurtured, treasured. But in an inner London school in 1994, it was dismissed as a social embarrassment, the equivalent of picking your nose in public. The girl took off her shoes and carefully put them over to one side before rejoining the back of the line. She slunk there, her hips at a surly angle, disdain in her eyes. Far from offering encouragement to help develop her natural ability, here was the girl's educational mentor telling her that her skill was unwanted, worthless. And then we wonder why Britain does not produce its share of athletes.

The head teacher, loudhailer in hand, though, seemed oblivious to the pain she had just inflicted and strode through the disappointed, distracted, uninterested throng as if she had in her possession the very key to youthful nirvana. As she walked through the teams, trilling about how marvellously everyone had done, kids would ask her continually: 'Who's winning?' It didn't matter how many times she answered, 'That's not why we are here, as far as we're concerned everyone is doing equally brilliantly', some child would always come back with a 'Yes, but which team's winning?' Eventually, as the last dribble of water had been poured into a bucket and the last coloured bar placed in its properly coordinated, coded position, she announced that it was all over. Immediately a chorus of voices chirruped: 'Who's won?' She ignored them, brushing aside the torrent of questions. Everyone, she announced, would receive a sticker for doing so well and everyone should be congratulated on completing the tasks together. It was all about teams, she insisted, working together, not against each other.

Before she could hand out the stickers, an intrepid parent came forward and asked if there would be that traditional staple of the school sports day: the parents' race.

'I don't think so,' she said. 'We don't go in for that sort of thing at this school.'

So, someone else asked, would there be any races at all?

'No races, no,' she said.

This provoked the sort of groan from the assembled children that not even she could misconstrue. They must have heard its low rumble in Sheffield.

'Please, can we have some races?' the older ones begged. A couple of the parents joined in the chorus. Within a second, a forest fire of pleading had broken out, children asking for races all round the field. But the head teacher was unswayed.

'We've finished for this morning, thank you.'

Eventually one of the teachers pointed out that there were some tennis balls used in a sorting game and there were spoons for the carrying-sand relay. Maybe we could have an egg-and-spoon race?

'No.'

'Puh-lease,' chorused the children.

'No.'

'Just this one race,' said the other teacher. 'We've got the time.'

Finally, with a shirty tut, the head teacher relented.

'OK, by popular demand we'll have an egg-and-spoon challenge.'

It was as if someone had just switched on the electricity. There was excited chatter everywhere. The girls came over from under the trees asking what was going down. Children began to pick up the spoons and tennis balls to practise their technique. And me, I took Hugo to one side and showed him how to hold them.

'Look,' I said. 'Just keep your thumb on the back of the ball. That way it won't fall off, see.'

'OK, Dad,' he said.

His race was the third one. In the first two, the noise was huge as the children and parents cheered on their favourites. Competition had broken out and you could feel its power coursing round the field. But despite the encouragement, nobody could quite master the balance of ball on spoon. No matter how much they stuck out their tongues to aid concentration, no matter whether they dashed off or took their time, the ball would just keep slipping off. I nodded at Hugo. He nodded back. When it was his turn, I watched him line up with a growing sense of optimism.

'Ready, steady, go,' shouted one of the teachers (the head was standing aloof from the fray, ostentatiously not getting involved, the loudhailer hanging down by her side).

And off Hugo went. As the others in the race were almost immediately picking up balls tumbling from spoons, Hugo streaked away, heading easily and smoothly towards the finishing line, a winner all the way. The fact that his left hand was cupped over his tennis ball holding it firmly into place a mere detail.

'Stop, stop,' the head teacher, suddenly taking an interest, shouted through her megaphone. 'Hugo, what on earth are you doing?'

She marched over to Hugo.

'Why are you holding the ball with your hand? Just explain why you were you doing that?'

And my son, rightly, told her what had happened, his tiny voice picked up by the loudhailer brandished in front of his mouth and echoing across the field.

'That's how my dad told me to hold it,' he said.

At which the head teacher looked at me, accusingly, disappointedly, angrily. She could not have looked more unhappy if I had just exposed myself. But in a sense I had. From now on the die was cast: I was a competitive dad.

1

It's started, then

Early Sunday morning and the phone is ringing for the third time. It is Paul's mum.

'What time's the game?' she says.

'We're at home. Meet at ten,' I say. 'I'm sure I told Paul at training.'

'Yeah, yeah, no, that's what he thought you'd said,' she says. 'But you know. Best to check.'

I put the phone down and look at the clock. It's 8.45. There is no point going back to bed and anyway I've been awake since about six, my mind crammed with formations and permutations, substitutions and possibilities. I've already had an internal debate about tactics (should we start with the best team? Or should we lull the opposition into a false sense of security by keeping Lee on the touchline then unleashing him, say, twenty minutes in?). I've rehearsed my half-time talk (roughly, 'Give it to Lee'). And I've told myself not to get involved if their parent linesman turns out to be flag-happy (after all, we don't want another incident like the one at Cranford last year so early in the new season).

I wander back into the bedroom to find some clothes and knock over something that skittles across the floor.

'It's started, then,' says a voice from within the bed.

'Yeah. Sorry.'

'I'll be glad when it's over,' the voice says.

'It's the first game of the season.'

'Exactly.'

The phone rings again.

'Howzit, it's Hamish, what time's kick-off?'

'We're at home, meet at ten,' I say. 'I thought I sent you an email.'

'Did you? Oh, OK, I haven't checked my emails for a couple of days. Anyhow, see you there.'

I put the receiver down, return to the bedroom, manage not to knock anything over and restart the search for my trousers. The phone rings. That'll be Hamish again.

'It's Hamish again. Sorry. Forgot to say: any chance you could pick Fraser and me up? Only Susie needs the car this morning. Tesco's.'

'Sure,' I say.

I find my trousers, wondering whether it might be time to wake Barney up. He is never at his best first thing in the morning, so I decide to leave it, let him get those last couple of moments' sleep in the hope it might make a difference. I'm just about to go into the kitchen as Hugo, eighteen and gadabout, comes out.

'Morning, you're up early,' I say to him, yet to latch on to the fact that he's fully clothed, still wearing the stuff I'd seen him in the night before.

'I've just got back,' he says. 'What are you doing?'

'Football,' I say. 'Season's starting today. Want to come and watch?'

'Nah,' he says, 'I'm just off to bed. See you.'

'Want a cup of tea?' I say, hoping to detain him for a few seconds of conversation.

'No, I'm all right.'

I make a cup for myself and, sitting at the kitchen table, start to write out today's team. I do this a lot. Most of my notebooks have a couple of pages of line-ups some-where. I was once interviewing a leading manager and my book fell open at a page of scribbled formations. I caught a glimpse of him looking at the line-ups and felt moved to explain: 'Teams. I coach boys' football. I expect you write out teams all the time too.'

'No,' he replied.

On this occasion, though, rather than write out the team, I realise it's quicker to list those who aren't avail-able. So I do. Rory: still on holiday. Franz: suffering from growing pains. Adam: playing cricket. Mark: it's his weekend with his dad in Reading. Luke: got repetitive strain injury in his wrist from playing on the PlayStation. It is not, I think, a list of selection issues likely to detain Arsène Wenger or Rafa Benitez. Except for the PlayStation one, obviously.

I then scribble the team down and find I've only got ten players. I can't work that out. There are sixteen in the squad and five aren't available. I run through the list again: just ten. I check the names: Max, Gio, Tim, Kal, Jamie, Paul, Fraser, Lee, Ryan and Faisal. That's ten, however you look at it, even if you turn the page upside down, which I do a couple of times. I go upstairs, get out my file of registration cards each player requires to play in league matches and try to work out who it is that is missing. It is a bit of a nostalgia trip, flicking through the cards. They date from the season we came together as a team when the boys were just eight. There's a photo on each of the cards and here's Kal, our now prematurely mature skipper, without a moustache. Here's Tim, our six-foot-something centre back, just a little boy. And look at Barney. I study the picture of him grinning at the camera, three gaps on his top row where teeth should have been, that sweatshirt he wore all the time, even when he went to bed. He is so small he is having to strain upwards in the photo booth to get his whole face in the frame. It only seems like last week that he looked like that and now he's nearly fourteen, an adolescent, approaching my height, with hormones and growth spurts and an uncanny ability to make any room he sleeps in smell of gerbils. I smile and put the cards back. Then it occurs to me who the missing player is: it's Barney. Bloody hell, I've forgotten my own son.

I go into his room. When he was a baby, I could spend ages just looking at him sleeping. He had this habit of suddenly sighing deep and long as if all the cares of the world were piled upon his nappy-clad form, whereas in reality all he had to worry about was whether his milk would arrive on time. I used to hang on after I'd kissed his forehead, just waiting for that sigh.

Today, thirteen and a bit years on, Barney is lying on his back, legs splayed, hands clasped fast to his groin, mouth open. There is a vague smell of gerbils in the room.

'Barns,' I say. 'Wake up. It's past nine. I'll put your kit out.'

I go to his cupboard and begin the search. It is packed in there, jungle-like, dense with T-shirts and jeans and hoodies, at least three quarters of which are now way too small for him. Rifling through the detritus, moving aside trousers that these days hang about three inches above his ankle bone, shirts with buttons that no longer reach across his chest, that eight-year-old's sweatshirt that's still being given cupboard room because his mother can't bear to throw it out, there is no sign of a red-and-white-striped football top, black shorts or two black socks. Never mind a pair of shin pads.

'Any idea where your kit is?' I say.

'Er . . . ?'

'Your kit.'

'In the wash?'

This is an exchange conducted without any evidence whatsoever that one of the participants is awake.

'Barns, you'd better get up.'

'Sorry?'

I head downstairs and start rummaging through the laundry basket. With three teenagers in the house, it is no minor task. His kit is at the bottom, beneath the crusty and the encrusted, the scuddy and the skiddy. When the team first started, we used to keep all the shirts together in one big bag to prevent them going astray and had a rota among parents to wash them. The idea had been abandoned when Sanjay, Kal's dad, turned up one Sunday, very apologetic.

'They were very muddy, so Gita thought she'd better put them through the boil wash,' he said. He then pulled from the bag a shirt. Its red and white stripes had merged into a single, delicate shade of pink.

'Are they all . . . ?' I said.

He nodded: 'I'm afraid so.'

For small boys, pink proved not to be a comfortable colour.

'It's because we all look like girls,' Fraser had said, by way of tactical analysis, after one sorry defeat. The pink look lasted three more matches before it was decided to invest in a new outfit. And after that everyone became responsible for their own stuff. As a solution this was still not wholly satisfactory. Luke contrived to lose his after only one game and had to spend the next two seasons pretty in pink. As it happens, in Barney's case, there was a never a chance of the colours running for the simple reason his kit never seems to get washed. He is either wearing it, or by some unspoken, unproven law of laundry, it finds its way to the nether reaches of the basket, where it remains unattended until the next time it is needed.

When I finally find it, unwisely I sniff the shirt: gerbils. I spray a bit of his brother's Lynx on it. I sniff it again. I'm not sure if this constitutes improvement. I take the kit upstairs.

'Barns, you up?'

'When's the game?'

'Ten. Sorted your boots?'

'Who we playing?'

'Littlebourne. Have you done your boots?'

'God, my mouth's really parched.'

'Your boots? Done them?'

'Yes.'

'Really?'

'No.'

I've been awake for hours, but somehow, as always seems to happen on a Sunday morning, we are now running late. I dash about collecting balls, first aid kit, pump to pump up the balls, shin pads, spare keeper's gloves in case Max forgets his, players' registration cards, mobile, car keys, pen, bibs, cones, water bottles. Plus Barney's boots, which still have the rugby studs in them. I find his football studs in a drawer and hand boots, studs and spanner to him as we scramble out of the door.

'You need to rehydrate,' I say. 'Get some water down

you. And have you eaten anything? Have a banana.'

It's nearly ten as I pile everything into the car: balls, bags, bottles, banana, Barney. We dash up the road to the club, for once slowing in time as we pass the speed camera stationed strategically behind a huge tree, an item which has caught me in a Sunday-morning ambush at least twice over the years.

We moved out of London ten years ago to one of the once distinct small cities on its borders that are daily being sucked closer to the sprawl. The club is in one of the plusher ends of town, in a park next door to a graveyard. A couple of years back, the council sent us notice to quit as they needed the open space to expand the yard; apparently they were running short of grave-space. There was a flurry of opposition from the swanky houses that flank the park, whose occupants came up with the neat rallying call of 'Facilities for the living, not the dead'. There was a public protest on the field, when a few of the lads turned up in full kit and mixed with a couple of placard-waving residents and the local MP. Someone said that the council would need even more space when everyone dies through being overweight because they can't play football; with decision-making like that, coffins can only get bigger. Everyone laughed and we made a lot of noise (rather more, you imagine, than the council's intended new tenants) and it was on the regional news. Without wishing to suggest that the council's thought process is dependent on what is on the BBC's 6.30 p.m. bulletin, soon afterwards the graveyard expansion plans were put on hold.

The campaign victory was the one occasion in the history of the club where its members have found common cause with the locals. Normally, the two parties are locked in semi-permanent verbal warfare about everything, but mainly the parking. You can understand why those who live nearby get upset: Sunday morning is the one time their expensively purchased silence is compromised.

There are three matches on this morning and already the road is filled with vehicles. Out of dozens of cars are pouring small boys and larger parents. Some parents are carrying enough kit for a month-long expedition to the Hindu Kush: flasks, folding chairs, gazebos, video cameras. Dogs and grandparents and younger siblings tag along. Just outside the clubhouse, a new SUV the size of a Chieftain tank has double-parked, its hazard warning lights flashing as if to legitimise the obstruction it is causing. A woman with Ray-Bans perched on top of a flourish of blonde hair opens the back door and a boy steps out. She kisses him on both cheeks.

'Good luck, Philo darling,' she says in a voice slightly louder than her son finds comfortable. 'I'll be along for the second half. And I've texted Daddy and he's promised he'll be here too.'

As she hands the boy his new Chelsea boot bag, a man in a baseball cap, three-quarter-length trousers and a Liverpool shirt is climbing out of a white van, still with decorator's ladders on the roof.

'Come on, Kyle,' he shouts. And a tubby little boy waddles around from the passenger door. He too carries a Chelsea boot bag. The two boys arrive at the gate into the park at the same time.

'A'right, Philo,' says Kyle.

'Oh hi, Kyle, hi,' says Philo.

They are both members of the club's under-elevens and as they greet each other, the democracy of boys' football swings into Sunday-morning action. This is the one place in the whole social fabric of our city where the offspring of the millionaires' villas to the north meet on the same footing as the lads from the housing estates to the east. On the touchline high-maintenance wives stand shoulder to shoulder with blokes they would otherwise encounter only if they employed them to redecorate their interiors. Here they are about to engage in a process in which privilege or position have no bearing. Here money can buy you nothing, except a lukewarm cup of tea. Here everyone starts equal.

Well, almost equal. This morning, I can't help noticing, there is a preponderance of white vans parked up along the street, which, according to the first law of Sunday-morning football, suggests that our opposition might start in a position slightly more equal than us.

We arrive to find all of our lot already there. Barry, Lee's dad and my co-coach, is making exaggerated pointing motions at his watch. A couple of the other dads join in, cheerfully.

'Sorry, guys,' I say. 'Sorry, my fault.'

The opposition, too, are here, fanning out across the pitch in formation, looking alarmingly organised. Their coach, who is wearing a tracksuit with the club's name on the back and his own initials embroidered on the chest, is drilling them through a series of warm-up exercises. They leap and jump and stretch and touch the ground in unison. On one exercise, they clap in time as they skip. On another, they shout out their team's name. Meanwhile, our lads are standing in a circle, pointing at Gio's new boots and laughing. The boots are yellow. Max comes up and tells me he has forgotten his gloves. I do a head count. Ten players. Someone's missing. I run through the team.

'Oh, bugger,' I say. 'I've forgotten to pick up Hamish and Fraser.'

Afterwards, as the boys gather round, looking crestfallen and disappointed while the opposition make their way to their dads' vans, chirpy in victory, I try out a line that I nicked from Alex Ferguson.

'That's the thing about the A League. Make a mistake in the B and you get away with it. Make a mistake up here and the roof will fall in on your head.'

Fergie was talking about the step up from the Premiership to the Champions League, but the point is much the same: the gap in class here in our under-fourteens league is enormous. I do that a lot, steal lines from the professionals. My Sunday-morning oratory is generally an unholy mix of Arsène and Alex, José and Rafa. I scour the quotes columns of the newspapers for usable phrases, make notes in the margins of autobiographies of telling little epithets, listen to what they have to say when being closely probed by Garth Crooks on *Match of the Day*. Though usually I have fallen asleep by the time he finishes his question.

You might think that what they have to say would have little relevance to a level of football as unsophisticated as this, but it is surprising how little things change verbally as you advance up the football pyramid. I once stood within earshot of John Gorman, then manager of Wycombe Wanderers, during a preseason friendly as he yelled out instructions to his players just before the opposition were about to take a corner.

'Mark, mark,' he was shouting. 'White shirt on a blue shirt. Everyone pick someone up and stick with them.'

And I thought, This bloke used to be assistant manager of England and I could have shouted that. In fact, I do shout it at virtually every game, so much so I'm pretty certain the boys have grown deaf to my instructions. They certainly have this morning as, not once but twice, they allowed an opponent to remain completely unmarked in the area as his team-mate prepared to take a corner.

'Mark him, mark the number-five,' I yelled from the touchline the moment I spotted a boy the size of a small tower block lumbering into exactly the same spot from which he scored the opening goal in the first half. 'Red shirt on a yellow shirt. Everyone pick someone up and stick with him.'

In the defence, there was a lot of pointing, a lot of delegating of responsibility, a lot of telling someone else to mark. Kal pointed at Jamie. Jamie pointed at Paul. Paul looked at Fraser. And Fraser pointed at Barney. Nobody, however, went anywhere near the big number-five. The ball did, though, and he headed the winner through Max's hands. And this after Lee had scored a wonderful equaliser, tricking his way past three of their defenders, and putting us within just five minutes of a point in our first-ever game in the top division.

'We lost here when we should have got at least a draw because we made defensive errors,' I continue. 'Not marking at corners. How often do we have to talk about that? Really, lads, how often?'

I realise my voice is tailing off into a pointless moan. I have lost eye contact with most of the players, who are now, almost to a man, looking at their feet. The exception is Tim who is looking at Gio and raising his eyes heavenwards. Thirteen-year-olds hear enough of this sort of adult tone at home ('How often do I have to ask you not to drink straight from the bottle?' and 'You were told to clean your room a week last Thursday and still you've

not done it' and 'How many times have you been told
to switch the lights off when you go to bed?'). So much
so, they have become experts at employing strategic deaf-
ness. I might as well be talking Swahili. Or whatever
language it is Big Ron uses. I change tack quickly.

'But we'll work on the mistakes and we'll eradicate
them. The encouraging thing is, everyone gave 100 per
cent. You all tried hard. And that sort of effort will get
rewards. Besides, in every way bar those two mistakes, you
matched them. Honestly, they wouldn't have had a sniff
if we hadn't made those errors. So, we're on our way, lads.
Well done, see you Tuesday.'

Barry claps his hands and says, 'Well done, lads, brilliant', and a couple of parents join in with a 'Great start'
or a 'Fantastic, boys, well done', and we break up giving
the impression to any passing neutral that we must have
just won the cup, rather than lost to a team that only just
avoided relegation last season. All that is left to do is take
down the nets, collect the corner flags, fill in the match
card, gather up the balls, put the water bottles back in
the carrying case, reunite several abandoned hoodies with
their owners, put the two hoodies that no one claims in
with the seventeen others in the lost property box in the
clubhouse and, finally, give the referee his fee.

'Twenty pounds?' I say. 'Bloody hell, it's gone up. For
that sort of money you expect at least a penalty.'

'Penalties cost double,' says the ref.

'Cheap at half the price,' I say.

'Forty a penalty, thirty-five a direct free-kick just outside
the box,' he says.

'We'll have a whip-round next time,' I say. Before
adding, in a whisper, 'By the way, are you serious?'

'No.'

There is an under-elevens game going on in the lower field as we make our way back to the car, and Barney and I stand and watch for a few minutes.

'Come on, lads,' he shouts.

Watching the under-elevens, it is remarkable how quickly the boys grow up. These guys look so small, so fragile. They all gather round the ball, hunting in packs; there is no perception of space, of seeking out the empty parts of the pitch to use to their advantage. On the touch-line, the two coaches yell and point. Suddenly, a tiny little boy emerges from the pack and heads towards the goal, running with an urgency few of his opponents can match. When he arrives at the edge of the penalty area, however, he seems unsure what to do and stops in the hope that one of his team-mates will have caught up with him. As he stands waiting for assistance, a defender wanders over and hoofs the ball out for a corner. There is much shouting from the touchline.

'Mark them, mark them. Yellow shirt on red shirt. Everyone pick an opponent and stick with them.'

As the ball floats over, several small boys shut their eyes and jump vaguely in its direction. They miss it. One of them is the goalkeeper. The ball lands about three feet from the goal line. Its arrival provokes a frenzy of fruit-less kicking. It pinballs around, bouncing from shin to shin, with no one able to apply a clean kick. On the touch-line, parents and coaches alike are whipping themselves into a frenzy screaming either 'Score' or 'Clear it' depending on their allegiance. The woman who earlier had deposited her boy from her SUV looks as if she may combust at any moment.

'Kick it, Philey, kick it. For Christ's sake kick the bloody thing.'

The ball eventually falls to the tiny boy, standing alone and unnoticed on the penalty spot. He smacks his shot home, causing delirious celebrations among the parents.

'It's amazing, looking at that, how much you lot have changed,' I say to Barney as we make our way back to the car.

'Not really,' he says. 'We're still crap at marking at corners.'

2

A health and safety issue

There is a dog shit problem. It is Sunday morning, I'm in the clubhouse, gathering up the nets, when Luke comes in, breathless, excited.

'It's steaming,' he says. 'Great big pile. Massive.'

'Where this time?' I ask.

'Right in the centre circle,' he says. 'Got to respect a dog that can pick its spot like that.'

I look about the clubhouse for the shovel, kept especially for such occasions, but I can't see it. I try the dressing rooms, the toilets, the referee's room, the little cupboard next to it that we somewhat optimistically call the trophy room: no sign of a shovel. Mike, the manager of the under-twelves, has arrived to set up for his game.

'Seen the shovel?' I ask.

'Dog shit?' he says. 'Where this time?'

'Centre circle, apparently,' I say.

'Bloody hell,' says Mike. 'He's got some shot on him, that dog. Have we signed him up yet?'

Mike hasn't seen the shovel and I can't find it anywhere, so I head out to the field armed only with a brush and a plastic cone. There is a small group of players and parents already gathered out in the middle. Luke has jogged ahead of me, anxious not to miss any of the fun. As I approach, I can see it from ten yards away. In the midst of the giggling, pointing group, a cairn of faeces rises up from the grass. Luke is right. It has been placed with geometric precision bang on the centre spot.

'It was on the penalty spot last week,' says Luke, who seems to have made a study of the issue, mapping canine discharge across the field.

'No, last week it was on the edge of the area,' says Rory now back from holiday and available for selection.

'No, that was last season. Definitely the penalty spot,' says Luke. 'There was still some left on it when my brother's team came to play. When they got a pen, the ref got into a right state because whoever was taking it wouldn't put it on the spot because he didn't want to get shite all over the ball.'

'Right, everyone,' I say, surveying the problem. 'Stand back. There's only one thing for it.'

I bend down and brush some of the pile into the cone. The surface crust disturbed, a putrid pong emerges from the depths which is greeted by exaggerated retching from several in the gathering crowd. Gingerly, holding it as if it might at any point explode, I carry the cone over to the hedge and try to toss the mess into the foliage. But it barely moves, sticking to the plastic surface like glue. Luke is on my shoulder.

'What does it eat, this dog?' he says.

I scrape as much off as I can, then wipe the cone on the grass, leaving a brown smear across the turf. As I walk back to clear the remaining pile, the referee has joined the growing circle of observers.

'Are you the manager? Health and safety issue. This will have to be properly removed. That won't do the job. You need a shovel.'

Mike is brilliant at delegating, and has given the parents of his under-twelves responsibility for all sorts of aspects of running the team, from filling the water bottles to completing the match card. Doubtless he has a shovel monitor who dutifully scours the pitches for invasive piles and deals with them accordingly, roping up and donning crampons to remove the little Everests from around the playing area. But for me, clearing shite is all part of the Sunday-morning duty. And I can't help thinking as I carry a second pile hedgewards, the cone bending under the weight and threatening to deposit its load all over my shoes, that José Mourinho probably doesn't include this in his list of managerial duties.

And it happens every week. The club has been in a condition of minor warfare with dogs for as long as I have been associated with it. It is not so much the actual creatures themselves that are the issue, though occasionally you do get a mad charger who dashes on to the pitch in the middle of a game in pursuit of the ball, scattering small boys in its wash. Once during one of our matches a couple of years back, the referee caught a crazed pup with a glorious, full-length diving rugby tackle.

'Look, it's Jimmy Greaves,' I'd said, thinking of that footage of Greavsie downing a mutt during the World Cup in Chile.

'Who?' someone had said.

'Jimmy Greaves. World Cup in 1962, caught a dog.'

'Who's Jimmy Greaves?' they asked.

I wouldn't have minded if it had been one of the boys. But it was a parent. When even the mums and dads are too young to get your cultural references, you know you're past it.

Greaves-style pitch invaders, though, are less of a concern than the deposits they leave behind. The locals have always exercised their mutts here and for years it was a mess whenever we came to use the pitches. At the very sight of a patch of green, the back legs of every four-legged visitor hereabouts would quiver with the delicious expectation of leaving their mark. It was an open dog sewer.

In a way, I couldn't blame the dog owners. When our lot were smaller, they all said they wanted a dog. My wife said she would only get one if they walked it and didn't leave it to her.

'Course we will,' said Ellie, my daughter.

So to test them we looked after a dog for a fortnight while his owner went abroad. Frank he was called, a nice mutt with a sweet nature. Not sweet enough for the children to bother walking him, but sweet nonetheless. And I was soon delegated walking responsibilities. We live in the middle of town, in among a load of churches and religious institutions. Every morning I'd take Frank out for his constitutional and he would unload his bowels on the doorstep of one of them. He was scrupulously ecumenical in his positioning: it was the Catholics one day, the Quakers the next. Every time, as he left his deposit on the pavement, I had to clear it up into a plastic bag. And clearly we hadn't been feeding him on what he had been used to at home, because it became runnier and wetter and more noxious as the days progressed. In the end, I was reduced to shoving him into the car and driving to a park nearby, pushing him out and letting him go. Here I could, with a swift glance over each shoulder to check no one was looking, leave his mess in situ.

Evidently our pitches were the haunt of every Frank in the neighbourhood. At one point, the club committee had seriously discussed buying some sort of outdoor vacuum cleaner to hoover up the sabbath deposits. Then our chairman persuaded the council to place a couple of pooper scoop bins by the entrance gate, and things improved as most owners conscientiously bagged and chucked. But for the last season or so we have been plagued by a phantom crapster, an owner who not only refuses to do any scooping, but appears to have unleashed an attack hound to set down strategically positioned piles. Their leavings are never on the touchline, or on the fringes of the midfield. They are never out on the wing or just over by the corner flag. They are always on a vital part of the pitch, placed to cause maximum drama, in a spot we cannot possibly miss. This is mess with a message.

I have my suspicions as to who might be responsible. Two seasons ago, my then co-manager Jeff was acting as linesman on the side of the pitch which abuts several gardens. A muscular clearance out of defence saw the ball flying out of the park and over a fence. Jeff went into the garden to retrieve it, leaving the gate open behind him. As he rummaged around in the undergrowth, a large, sleek dog dashed out through the open gate and bounded off across the park. A couple of moments later, Jeff emerged with the ball and shut the gate behind him. He was followed in close order by the dog's owner, red in the face, yelling. He could not have been more animated if Jeff had just trampled his prize begonias. From across the other side of the pitch, I couldn't quite catch what was being shouted, but the man concerned was now bearing down on Jeff, who was attempting to return to his flagsman's duties. But his efforts were badly compromised when the man caught up with him and started hitting him about the chest with a pair of gardening gloves. It looked like a challenge to a duel being issued by an enraged Alan Titchmarsh. By now, together with Barry, I was on my way round the pitch to Jeff's assistance. As we neared we could hear the gist of his assailant's complaint.

'She's on heat. She's pedigree, rare breed, lineage as long as your bloody arm, she's off to stud tomorrow,' he was yelling. 'And you, you idiot, let her out. Now any old fleabag can get at her. You'll have cost me thousands.'

'Leave it out,' Jeff was saying. 'There's a match going on. I'm the linesman.'

'I don't bloody care if you're Graham bleeding Poll,' said the man. 'If my dog gets pregnant because of you, I want compensating.'

I tried to step into the fray.

'We'll get her back for you,' I said to the owner. 'I'm sure it's not as bad as that.'

'Oh really?' said Barry. 'Take a look over there.'

And, sure enough, over by the copse which separates the park's two pitches, we could see the prize bitch was already being serviced by a scruffy looking mongrel wearing on its leering, busy little face the look of someone who had just scooped the Euro Lottery on rollover week. Nothing like a bit of posh totty.

'Oh shit,' said Jeff.

'Yes exactly,' said the man. 'Oh shit.'

Only a few months after that the crap piles began to appear. I have absolutely no proof but it has long been my suspicion that the pedigree bitch's owner got his revenge by feeding the resultant crossbreed offspring on some military strength laxative and then training them up to do their business on our playing surface. Somehow, it could only have happened to Jeff.

This morning, things do not much improve after the pre-match incident on the centre spot. In fact, shovelling shit is the highlight of my morning. We are guffed 6-1 in a performance which suggests things in the A League are going to be very tricky indeed. True, there are extenuating circumstances. Our opponents were league runners-up last year, so must be reckoned a bit on the useful side. Plus Kal, our captain and guiding influence, hobbles off after no more than five minutes with an ankle injury that does not look minor. And Paul, his partner in central midfield and a talented little all-round sportsman, isn't playing at all, he's off with the county rugby squad, or the South of England hockey team or at indoor cricket nets, or something. Plus the referee disallows a perfectly good equaliser from Lee which would have made it 2-2 at half-time and could have changed the direction of the game.

But mainly we lose because our team members are not all over six foot tall.

It is a central fact of adolescent sport that boys develop at different speeds. You can see the imbalance every Sunday morning: booming-voiced giants play in the same team as piping-voiced midgets. In development terms, boys of the same age can be five or six years apart. Manchester United's Norman Whiteside, for instance, was renowned for being a fully formed monster at the age of thirteen, a man-child who stomped and snarled around the junior circuit, winning matches by sheer force of physicality almost from the point he could walk. Mark Hughes, not himself exactly a retiring physical presence on a football field, recalls how once, playing for the Wales schoolboy

team against Northern Ireland, the Welsh side had cowered
in the changing room at half-time, asking each other what
they had done in their lives to deserve being confronted
by the monstrous apparition that was the young Whiteside.
Liverpool's Jamie Carragher, on the other hand, was a late
developer, a little boy amongst men until he finally hit
puberty at sixteen. Nobly, his club stuck by him as he
grew, allowing him to reach his full potential as a professional footballer: missing a penalty for his country in the
quarter-final of the 2006 World Cup.

Team photos of most under-fourteen teams reveal a
couple of lads who look as though they could be served
in pubs standing alongside a couple more who look as if
they should still be in primary school. We have it in our
side: Tim and Gio, little and large, inseparable mates off
the pitch, yet one barely reaches his friend's shoulder.

In youth football at every level size matters. In my
twenties the team I used to run in London included a
Scottish bloke called Gerry. No instrument had yet been
invented to measure pace as slow as Gerry's. He would
lumber around up front, failing to reach through balls,
invariably caught in possession, occasionally falling over
his own feet. In short, he was no better than the rest of
us. Yet he had claimed before he joined that he had been
Celtic's youth team centre forward, indeed that he had
kept Brian McClair out of the Bhoys' under-fourteens.
We were so excited by the prospect of a proper player
joining our ranks that we didn't even bother to give him
a trial; in he came, replacing Simon the barrister up front
without so much as a judicial hearing. We were soon
disabused. Watching him failing to do anything other than
complain about the service he was receiving every week,
the suspicion soon took root that he was a fantasist.

'Which Celtic did you say you played for, Ger?' someone had asked in the pub after one particularly clueless perform-ance. 'Stalybridge Celtic?'

Eventually a cynic in the team (it might have been me) contacted the Celtic archivist in Glasgow to find out if this Gerry bloke had ever played for the club. Astonishingly, he had. Not once, either, but many times. And yes, he was a contemporary of Brian McClair's. But the thing was, he had been six foot odd aged thirteen. He scored hundreds of goals in kids' football in Glasgow, merely by dint of being huge. He would crush defences, stamp on opposition, send smaller opponents flying across the red gravel pitches they insist on using up there. All his team-mates needed to do was to hoof the ball forward and Gerry's bulk would do the rest. He played for Celtic for three years, until everyone else caught up with him, and his scale could no longer compensate for minor failings such as a total lack of pace. Mind you, he was good company and, after four pints, did a great impression of Billy Connolly, so we let him stay in the team. Besides, even though he could barely run, could hardly kick and rarely hit a shot on target, he was a lot better than Simon.

Our opponents today are a team made up solely of English Gerrys. There are no squeaky voiced pre-adoles-cents to compensate for the lumbering giants. Thirteen, these lads? I'm not for a moment suggesting their manager is cheating the system by fielding over-age players, but I swear I see one of them after the game getting into the driver's seat of his car and heading off with his wife and kids to the pub for lunch. At least three of them sport more stubble than George Michael.

Sadly, confronted by such physical scale, lacking the midfield guile of Kal and spite of Paul, too many of our lads wilt. They disappear. They long for the final whistle to put them out of their temporary misery, to let them get back to less fraught things, like the PlayStation or MTV. They just don't want to know.

Alex Ferguson defines bravery on a football field as not so much putting your head in where others fear to put their feet, but wanting the ball when things are going wrong. He always cites Steve McManaman as one of the bravest players he ever saw. Not physically strong, perhaps, but never one to shirk in the bad times from the responsibility of possession. McManaman always wanted the ball, however rubbish his team was playing. And when you end your career with Manchester City that takes some doing. Today, it is clear, there are four or five of our team who are not Steve McManaman; they would rather the ball went anywhere other than near them. When we were in the B League, playing sides significantly less physical than today's opponents, the boys would be ravenous for possession, calling out their names all the time, pleading to be found by a pass and cutting rival defences to pieces with their confidence. Now, at one point during this game, when Max the keeper has the ball, I can see at least half the team look the other way, or pretend to tie their shoelace, or simply inspect the ground for any lingering evidence of dog shite: anything rather than attract his attention. Long before the end, as our huge opponents are swaggering through the midfield, the traffic exclusively one-way, most of our lads are hoping for a mercy killing to put them out of their misery and their embarrassment. It is not much of a way to spend a Sunday morning.

One thing is for sure: it is difficult to know what to say once the final whistle has sounded and I have shaken hands with the smirking rival manager, the referee and

their captain, who nearly puts his back out he has to lean
down so far to take my hand. Maybe I should just gather
up my things and walk away, say nothing and let my
silence speak volumes. Probably the best thing would
simply have been to gather everyone round and simply
announce: 'Not your day, boys. See you all at training on
Tuesday.' Undoubtedly the least useful, most pointless,
stupid and unproductive thing at this point would be to
lose my temper and unleash a volley of sarcasm at them.
Which is what I do.

'That was pathetic,' is my opening line. 'I can only think
from watching that pile of crap that you all want to go
straight back down to the B League. Well, if you want to
beat fat plonkers who can barely run never mind play
football 18-0 every week then fine. Great, let's all sink
back to that level. Or I tell you what, I'll buy eleven
plastic dustbins and we can play them. Though to be
honest, the way some of you played today, the wheelie
bin up front would score a bloody hat-trick.'

Even now, if I keep it general and don't target indi-
viduals for public criticism, there might be some profit
to be gained from such a verbal assault. The absolutely
indefensible thing to do, however, would be to pick out
anyone. They all feel small enough as it is.

'Luke,' I shout. 'Were you playing out there? Because
I didn't notice.'

This is not fair. I did notice Luke. At one point he had
attempted to mark their centre forward at a corner. Such
was the comical discrepancy in size, his dad had loudly
suggested from the touchline that he should take a set of
stepladders out on to the pitch just to even things up.
Luke had bravely flung himself at his opponent as the
ball came over and bounced off as if he had just made

contact with a six foot trampoline. In fact, Luke was by no means the worst. But it is he who bears the brunt of my invective. Maybe because, even as I apparently lose all sense of rationality, I retain just enough common sense to know he has the mental resolve to take it. Other boys, even if they are more culpable, would be crushed by being singled out. Luke hardly seems to notice. A couple of minutes after I have dismissed them with a curt 'See you Tuesday', I spot him charging off with his brother across the lower pitch, in search, no doubt, of more dog mess.

It would be good to suggest that a defeat like this is quickly forgotten. That perhaps I could face up to failure with equanimity, dispatching it into the memory bin within minutes. Maybe now, in the middle of my fifth decade of life experience, I should be mature enough not to let a minor setback like this cloud the rest of my day, my week, my month. Yeah, as if. We drive home in silence, Barney and me, with just some big band jazz oozing out of the car radio. When he doesn't even complain about me listening to Michael Parkinson on Radio 2, we know we are both in deep. We arrive home and he is first into the kitchen while I put the balls and stuff out the back. As I walk into the room, I just catch him making a gesture to his mother involving holding his nose and miming the pulling of a toilet chain.

'Oh dear, Dad, another day, another defeat,' says Ellie, the apprentice queen of sarcasm, as I follow behind into the kitchen. 'Six-one, not very good, is it?'

'I don't want to talk about it,' I say, trying to busy myself with laying the table in the fond hope that domestic business might be mistaken for getting on with my life. 'But that bloody referee . . .'

And off I go, listing the injustices stacked up against us, the ref, their linesman, the size of their centre forward, the fact that the ball was a bit soft, until the point where I become aware that I am addressing an empty room. I doubt even Barney is interested in this sort of analysis. Actually, there is no doubt: he isn't. While defeat hurts him, it is soon forgotten. As I stomp around, I can hear him and Ellie sniggering out in the hall, doing impressions of Basil Fawlty: 'Don't mention the score.'

Even as my children mock, there is another thing at work in my mind: guilt. The way I handled things was as poor as our marking for their first goal. It is in such circumstances, when things have gone badly for a team, that a coach shows his true colours. And mine appear to be a muddy shade of brown. What on earth was I doing, I say to myself as I fill the water jug, shouting at them like that? Frankly, faced with a boy at least seven inches taller than you charging around like something let loose on the streets of Pamplona, who can blame some of the lads for shrinking. I remember my own junior days on the lacrosse fields of Manchester and recall doing my best to dig a private hole out on the wing into which I could crawl when the going got tough. What was I doing laying into Luke? What crime had he perpetrated other than being small? It is at times like this, I think to myself, a migraine beginning to spread up my neck into the back of my head and across to my forehead, that you wonder why you do it.

Though Brian Moore, the former England rugby hooker, once told me that it is for precisely times like this that you do engage in sport. According to Moore, most of modern life is one long compromise. As a city solicitor during his playing days he would spend his time in the office fudging and conciliating, giving and taking, seeking the common ground. He couldn't wait for Saturdays and the chance to spend the afternoon with his head embedded between a pair of hairy thighs. For six days a week, he said, he lived in a perpetual fog of grey. Then on the seventh he had a glorious release into a world sharply defined in black and white.

He was right: out on the football field there is no negotiation of position, goals are not scored by rote, the man of the match award is not gifted by time-serving. The aims are simple and clear and you either achieve them through your own efforts or you don't: no one gives you anything. Unless you are playing against Northmeadow Youth Under-Fourteens that is, when you can usually rely on a goal being conceded from non-existent marking at a corner.

It also follows that if nothing in the rest of our comfortable, clinical, clean lives gives the same buzz as sporting victory, then nothing stings like sporting defeat. And today I sting as if I have just sat on a very large, very angry, very determined hornet. Attempting to make sure you don't ever feel this bad again is the biggest motivating vehicle known to man. Defeat is as important a thing as victory; it is part of the reason we play. You strive to win just so you don't have to lose.

Snappy and grumpy, introspective and taciturn, the depression governs my mood through the afternoon and evening and on into the next day. Indeed, it is still lingering as I arrive for training on Tuesday night. Barry, though, has a plan. His view is that it doesn't matter how big the opposition are, if we are fitter than them they'll never catch us.

'Stands to reason,' he explains. 'If we can keep on running for the full eighty minutes chances are they can't and we'll get the rewards in the last few minutes.'

As a strategy it does have some logic. Especially since, though they might be short in stature, we have plenty of willing, leather-lunged players in the team. Get them super fit and they might just have within them the last-minute spurt to win us a few necessary points. Without a square millimetre of fat on him, Barry himself is the paradigm of what fitness can do for a man. A scaffolder by trade, currently engaged constructing sets in a film studio, he has a physique honed by years of tough work. When he hangs by one hand from the crossbar untying the nets after a game, he can draw bigger applause from a Sunday-morning crowd than the football does. Once when we turned up for training on the municipal floodlit pitches down the road, there was a gang of fifteen-year-olds playing on the pitch we'd booked. I asked them to move because it was now our session, but they just scowled at me. I grabbed one of them by the arm, and they surrounded me, poking me in the chest, telling me I was out of order.

'You is out of order, know what I'm saying?' one of them said.

As I stood there, with not an idea in my head what to do next, Barry arrived. He wandered over and told me to walk away: he would handle it. I don't know what he said to them, but the youths quickly dispersed. It's called respect. He has it. I don't. Either that or he told them I was a practising paedophile with a penchant for fifteen-year-old chavs.

The first thing he does at this training session is a stretching exercise. I join in to show willing. We all stand, me and some dozen or so thirteen-year-olds, with our legs apart and attempt to grasp our ankles. I am easily the worst, just managing to reach my knees as I bend, my hamstrings about as yielding and supple as American foreign policy. Several of the boys have no problems at all. But Barney, I can't help noticing, has inherited his father's lack of flexibility and is making exaggerated groaning noises, his back barely bending.

'Come on, Barney,' says Barry, who is not only touching his toes, he has grabbed them in his fists and has put his head somewhere south of his shinbones. 'You can get down there.'

Barney huffs, puffs and falls over. Luke laughs. Next we move on to a hip flexor stretch which has everyone rolling around feigning agony, though in my case there is no feigning. Then we stretch our calves, our Achilles tendons, our shoulders, plus several muscles I was unaware I had. Ten minutes of this and memories of Sunday's defeat are consigned to a time when I wasn't feeling as if someone had just showered my calves in red-hot barbecue briquettes. And that is just the beginning.

'Good, now you're warmed up, we can start,' says Barry.

He soon has us jogging in single file round the penalty area, with the man at the back obliged to sprint past everyone to the front, an exercise repeated ad nauseam which leaves me gasping for air. There follows dashes and darts, quick-fire sprints and relays, all of them undertaken by the boys with a competitive relish. There is no shirking, no holding back, they plunge into the exercise in a manner which utterly belies their tame surrender on Sunday. But then, Barry has them on an incentive. The worst performer over the course of the session is obliged to undertake a forfeit. And today's forfeit has been chosen by Luke.

'I'll let him explain,' Barry said at the start of the evening.

'Well,' Luke said. 'It's easy, whoever comes last has to do twenty press-ups over this . . .'

And he led us all to a little hillock of freshly laid dog turd, steaming like a funeral pyre, rising out of the turf smack bang in the middle of one of the goalmouths. The thought of the loser's punishment is driving everyone on. In the sprints timings are followed with relish, the table of overall standings calculated with mathematical precision. As we reach the final event of the evening, the positions have sorted themselves out. We have all been given points for where we have finished in each event and already the quick lads like Ryan, Lee, Paul and Tim are in the clear, so far ahead of the slowcoaches that they could do the final stage on their hands and knees and still go nowhere near the dog shit. Mark, Luke and Adam have all done well, too. Franz was in trouble until a brilliant run in the three-cones relay pulls him out of turd contention. Fraser, Faisal and Gio have accumulated just enough points not to worry. In fact, as Barry marks out the course round which we all have to run, it is clear the competition for last place is between just two of those taking part: Barney and me. It is father against son for the right not to have to do twenty press-ups over a pile of dog mess.

In the past, I have always beaten him in races. Or at least I have always felt that I can, sometimes falling behind judiciously to allow him the confidence-boost of a win. But in this summer's beach Olympics on the glorious sandy stretch of Whitesands Bay in Pembrokeshire, the one in which Hugo, Ellie, Barney, several of their cousins and assorted hangers-on annually compete in such disciplines as rock shot put and seaweed discus, I noted that he was getting quicker all the time, his legs stretching and powering up to the point where Hugo really had to dig deep to beat him and retain elder brother status in the fifty-metre dash. Now he was up against me.

To ratchet up the tension, Barry puts us last. I stand and watch as Ryan and Tim and the rest glide round the course, turning sharply past cones, swivelling round the goalposts, making speed look effortless. All of the boys seem so much quicker and more coordinated than last year. They are beginning to lose the gawkiness of youth and are developing into a pretty close approximation to athletes.

It is my turn to go second last. Barry holds the stop-watch and the boys gather round him, counting me down as if for an execution. I belt out of the blocks, tear round the cones, as they chant, clap and jecr. I fall over the finish line, lungs burning.

'Thirty-seven point two seconds,' announces Barry. Ryan has done it in thirty-two. 'All Barney has to do is beat that to put you last.'

The boys are now in a frenzy of excitement, Luke in particular thrilled at the prospect of his coach being obliged to carry out his specially honed punishment. After a communal countdown from twenty, Barney heads off round the course. In the past, he has been one of the slower players in the side, making up in positional play what he lacks in pace. But today he has an incentive. He hurls across the turf, skimming past cones, driven on by his team-mates' chanting of his name. He powers home and falls over the line, his chest heaving with the strain.

'Barney, you have completed the course in . . .' says Barry, milking the moment for drama like he's presenting some celebrity reality TV show, '. . . thirty-seven . . . point . . . one seconds.'

Cue pandemonium. Barney is buried under a scrum of Tim, Gio, Rory and Fraser. Everyone is laughing. Luke can hardly contain his glee. Revenge is soon to be his.

And, as I make my way over to the scene of my forfeit, even as I squat over the pile and begin the twenty press-ups, wheezing and wobbling as I go, I think: Do you reckon, when he got his dog to foul up our lawns, the owner of the phantom shiter would have had any inkling of the positive effect his canine effluence would have on the team spirit of the under-fourteens?

3

The modern-day scoutmaster

We are at a dinner party and the bloke at the end of the table has opinions. After whipping through the condition of the government, the state of education and the upward march of property prices down his street, he has turned his attention to boys' football. It is, he says, an absolute disgrace. A joke.

'Got a boy?' he says. 'Well, whatever you do, don't get him into it.'

'Well, as a matter of fact—' I try to say.

'Seriously,' he insists, 'it's tantamount to child abuse.'

'Actually, I—'

'You're a journalist, aren't you? You ought to expose what's going on.'

'Well, the thing is—'

But there is no stopping him. Off he goes about how his lad had briefly played for a local club a few years back and how the whole thing was a bloody scandal. The facilities were ramshackle, the training amateurish, matches were war zones and really I shouldn't get him started on the coach in charge of it all.

'I think I should tell you—' I say, but it is like trying to derail an express train with a matchstick. His head of steam is up. He is now at full verbal gallop.

'I mean, how can any responsible organisation let a bloke like that loose on kids?'

This man was, he claims, a borderline psychotic: he swore as a matter of course, he yelled at the boys, he abused opponents and referees alike, he engaged in quite blatant cheating and foul play. And to cap it all he smoked on the touchline.

'Anyhow,' the bloke continues, 'you have to wonder who these people think they are. You know, screaming and carrying on and having a go at the referee like it's the most important thing in the world and in fact it's just a bunch of ten-year-olds trying to kick a ball around. What are they doing, these people?'

By now, we are in way too deep for me to reveal that I am one of these people. Instead, I nod and say something like:

'Sad little man syndrome, basically.'

'Exactly,' he says and pauses. And I think, Phew, that must be the end of it. I might just have got away with that. But no . . .

'Actually,' he starts up again, 'I think it's worse than sad little man syndrome. I guess since all those Scout leaders started to get exposed, it's about the only place the paedo can get access to kids these days.'

'I don't know about that, do you really—'

'Oh come on, there are tons of stories in the paper every year about men coaching kids. You have to think they're getting some sort of kick out of it. Why else do it? It's such a dangerous imbalance of power, you know, kids will do anything to curry favour. Honestly, they've got to be dodgy, haven't they? You really have to examine the motives of anyone involved in kids' football.'

At this point I try to move the subject on to something less personally contentious – the performance of Virgin trains, perhaps, or the pointlessness of Channel 5. But just as I am about to say something, at the other end of the table there has been a momentary lull in conversation and my wife catches the last two words of his diatribe drifting across the crockery.

'Kids' football?' she says, leaning over towards the bloke. 'Don't get him started on kids' football.'

'Too late,' he says, 'we were just talking about it, seems we're in total agreement.'

'Oh right,' she adds, and I think, Oh dear God, whatever you do, don't say it. Please don't say it. Just don't say it.

But she does.

'So you coach a team as well, do you?'

There is a pause.

'As well?' he says.

'Yeah,' she says. 'As well as him. He runs Barney's team. Has done for years. Loves it. Obsessed by it.'

The information hangs for a moment in the air. Down our end of the table there is a pause not so much pregnant as about to deliver triplets in a birthing pool without recourse to an epidural. The woman sitting opposite me looks at her plate and pushes gently at the little pile of butternut squash puree on it. Her fork scrapes against the crockery. The noise echoes down the table. I smile faintly. The bloke looks at me for a moment, long enough for me to catch the disdain in his eye, then he turns to the woman on his right.

'I saw you were driving a Peugeot,' he says. 'You didn't

get it from Junction Garages, did you? Bloody joke they are . . .'

No one says anything to me for what seems an age. I have been outed as a member of a pariah class, a social disaster zone. Will anyone, I wonder as I listen to him loudly complaining about pushy salesmen and the ridiculous cost of an annual service, ever speak to me again?

Then, as we are leaving, as the goodnights and thank yous and doorstep air kisses are being exchanged, I come face to face with the bloke once more over the coats.

'I, er, I . . . that's mine there,' I say, pointing at my jacket.

'Look,' he says. 'I didn't mean to suggest . . .'

'No . . .'

'I mean, I'm sure you're not . . .'

'No, course you . . .'

'I expect you're exemplary.'

'Well, I wouldn't exactly—'

'One thing, though,' he says as he hands me my jacket. 'Just let me ask you a question: who do you do it for? For the kids? Or for yourself?'

It is, I think as we make our way home, not a bad question. What I have always told myself is this: I'm doing it for my boy and his mates. That's how I got involved in the first place, wasn't it? Since he was four, Barney had been playing football every Saturday morning in a kickaround organised by two sixth-formers from the local school. They would charge parents £2.50 a time for what was not a lot more than a couple of hours babysitting with a ball. Sometimes there could be more than fifty kids there; this was the best paying Saturday job in town. Barney went along every week with his chum Fraser. In his little boots and postage stamp-sized replica shirt, he would tear round the pitch, madly committed, insanely keen, red-faced with effort. And just occasionally, coincidentally, he would come into contact with the ball.

But these lads were only prepared to look after kids under eight; older than that, they reckoned, they got too boisterous to control. So when he turned eight, one Saturday morning I took him to an open session at our local boys' league club, Northmeadow Youth. He went along with Fraser, and I stood on the touchline with his dad. Hamish was a natural enthusiast, who maintained an unending stream of encouragement like: 'Keep at 'em' or 'Never give up' or occasionally, when his excitement galloped ahead of his vocabulary, just a heartfelt: 'Grrrr . . . rrg'.

The set-up was altogether bigger. There were other age groups there. A match was in progress on the upper pitch, there were bibs, cones, goalposts. And a tea bar, from which Hamish bought me lukewarm coffee. It felt like a graduation, a seamless move up the football educational ladder. Most of all, Barney enjoyed himself, so I took him along to another session, then another. They were being conducted by a bloke with a raking smoker's cough who turned out to be Doug, the club chairman. For some reason, he called Barney Boris. On the fourth Saturday, Doug gathered the half-dozen parents together at the end of the session and told us that he didn't have time to run this group and that if a dad – or mum, no one could accuse him of being sexist, he said – didn't step forward and volunteer to take it on, he would have to disband it and there would be no football at all for our lads. As he said it, unlike everyone else gathered round, I must not have been looking with sufficient focus at my feet.

'Good, so you'll do it?' he said to me.

I didn't react.

'I said, so you'll do it?'

'Me?' I said.

'Well, do you want there to be football for these lads or not? Simple question, really.'

'Obviously I do, yeah, I mean . . .'

'So?'

'Well, OK, I'll think about it.'

As we were walking away, Hamish told me someone had to do it.

'The boys love it. We can't let it go.'

'What about you?' I said.

'Ah man, I would, but I'm up to my eyes just now. Anyhow, I never played soccer at school. Back home it was just rugby. They need proper coaching at this age. You'd be perfect. Tell you what, you coach them, I'll back you all the way.'

Thus was I trapped. The following week, as we arrived at the ground, I told Doug I was prepared to do it. I had a list of conditions I'd thought of on the way there. But he never gave me a chance to air them. Soon as I told him, he looked at his watch, pulled his car keys out of his pocket and started to walk away.

'Great,' he said. 'You can start now. There's some balls and cones in the clubhouse. I've got to dash. And watch that Boris. He's trouble.'

It was madness when I look back on it. No Criminal Records Bureau check, no coaching qualifications, just chuck me a bag full of balls and let me get on with it. Subsequently I learned that this was a trick Doug pulled at the start of every season. Tony, Paul's dad, found himself running his older boy's group under exactly the same circumstances. In this way, across the country are indulgent parents, anxious to ensure their offspring are not disappointed, suckered into management. It is the reluctant duty of fatherhood. Or at least that was what I told my wife.

'Come off it,' she said. 'You're desperate to do it. You'll love it.'

In a sense she was right. It was true, I had always wanted to be in charge of a team, to plot a campaign, plan it, maybe even win it. As an adolescent, I would spend hours taking myself through imaginary seasons in charge of United, or guiding Altrincham from the Northern Premier League to the European Cup. Pre-dating those Championship Manager computer games by about twenty-five years, I'd write out sheets of tightly annotated script detailing the seasons. It was all there: the transfers, the wheeler-dealings, the boardroom takeovers, the triumphs and failures. At first, I introduced an element of chance into proceedings, rolling dice to give me match scores. But then I thought too many 6-5 results just undermined the authenticity. Besides, with dice how do you get a goalless draw? So I manipulated things myself. And to prevent my career being one long procession of glory, I'd inflict bankruptcy on my teams, or scandal, or on one ghoulish occasion, a Munich-style air crash which wiped out the whole squad and forced me to move once more into my imaginary transfer market.

'What's all this?' my dad said to me once, catching me on the bed in my room surrounded by scribblings and jottings when I was supposed to be revising for exams. 'Is that what they call modern maths?'

The fantasy league eventually stopped, as I recall, not long after girls began to appear on my horizon. But though I put the pen down, the urge to plan and plot and pick my own teams didn't go away. After a while it found a

less theoretical outlet. Soon after I left university and moved
to London for work, I was calling a bunch of mates together
for kickarounds on Hampstead Heath. Word got out among
those who fancied a game and one summer's evening,
forty blokes turned up. In the pub afterwards a few of us
got chatting and, in that irrevocable law of boozing, as the
beer went down, so the ambition increased. By the end
of the evening, we had devised a seven-team league, playing
Friday nights on the floodlit AstroTurf pitches round inner
London.

My team was made up of mates from school, university, work and the pub. I bought kit for us, retro United
shirts with the initials WWFC printed on the chest. The
'WW' stood for Wordsworth Walk, the street where several
of us lived in a rented house. But after one game, a hopeless, cack-footed defeat, filled with recrimination and
complaint, as I shook hands with an opponent, he looked
at the shirt and said:

'What does that stand for? Willy Wanker's Football
Club?'

The name stuck, and we played for years after that,
proud Wankers all. People say the worst bit of organising
a football team is getting everyone together, making sure
there are enough players for a game. But I never minded
doing that, calling mates and mates of mates to corral
them along. Sometimes we struggled for numbers, sometimes we were oversubscribed. Slowly, we grew stronger:
good players came and brought their friends who were
even better. Some nights we sang; really at times it was
almost football that was being played out there. And the
best thing was, even if I was crap (and I was), nobody
begrudged me my place in the line-up because I organised it all. Plus I washed the shirts at the end of the match.

This was my team. I was the boss. After a couple of seasons, before games and at half-time, I started giving the team talks. Bob, the best player we had by a mile, generally added a few observations after I had finished. Oddly, while I had difficulty holding their attention, the lads always listened to his every word.

Still, I relished the fact that I was, albeit by default, in charge. One August I went out for a drink with Simon the barrister, who had been a regular Wanker until big Gerry the supersized Glaswegian turned up, blocking out all available light.

'Tell me,' Simon said, 'am I going to be playing for you this season or not?'

'Mate,' I said, 'you very much figure in my plans.'

'I'll take that as a no then,' he said.

And he was right.

So it continued from there. I sorted fixtures, organised transport, booked pitches and best of all, picked the teams. I kept detailed statistics on my PC, nominated man of the match, handed out player of the year awards. One time I even arranged an end-of-season dinner. Not everyone turned up, it has to be said. But Simon did. He only came, he confessed to me several years later, because he thought it might be the best way to ingratiate himself back into my plans.

So you could say, when Doug collared me that day to take charge of the Northmeadow Youth Under-Eights, it was my destiny. Which, if nothing else, proves the paucity of my destiny. But in truth, lurking at the back of my mind there was another reason why I was prepared to take on Barney's team. It stemmed from my experience watching my older son play.

On a football pitch, as everywhere else in life, Hugo is a very different character from his brother. Barney is a trier, full, as he enters adulthood, of increasingly muscular effort and jaw-clenched resolve. A boy who wouldn't give up if he was losing 15-0 with ten seconds to go, he is the footballing equivalent of Monty Python's limbless Black Knight, shouting, 'Coomon then', when reduced to just a torso. Hugo, on the other hand, is less inclined to toil. He is blessed with a lovely touch, can effortlessly do a Cruyff turn or a Matthews shimmy. He also enjoys a rich imaginative life, which occasionally gets in the way of his application; he mistakes thinking he has done something for actually doing it. I remember once, when he was eight, watching him in action. He was playing up front and spent much of the game standing in the centre circle engaged in a series of extravagant air kicks, turns and shimmies, followed by mimed goal celebrations. Towards the end of a game in which he had seen precious little, if any, of the ball, it finally fell kindly for him in the penalty area. Here was a chance to enact all those little bits of role play, to celebrate for real. I was on my toes with excitement; as the play unfurled it was evident my boy was going to do it. But he didn't seem to see the ball land at his feet, his eye was elsewhere. He made no attempt to kick it, never mind to try out any of the elegant manouevres he had been practising. The ball was quickly cleared and his chance went. The groan from the watching parents was a stinging soundtrack.

As we were driving home, I asked him what had happened and he said he hadn't seen the ball coming. Really, he hadn't. Just never saw it. By the time he realised it was there, it was gone. He had, he added, been too busy rehearsing in his mind what he would do if he scored the winning goal actually to score it. I can't tell you how much I wanted to lean across the gear stick and hug him when he said that. It was so sweet, it made my eyes water.

Now I accept that for a manager it is a lot easier to coach a team of Barneys than one of Hugos. It is a long-standing instinct of English football to favour the trier over the maverick, the lung-buster over the laconic. I know myself that defeat is a lot more acceptable if everyone has given of their all. It still hurts, but not quite as much.

But I can't forgive how Hugo was treated when he played. All a boy of nine or ten wants is to play football. Or in Hugo's case, to role-play football. But the coach in charge of the team he joined seemed to have lost sight of this simple truth. His priority was not helping the boys who turned up to have a good time, what he wanted was to win the league. He would go on scouting missions to watch other clubs, poaching the best existing talent from miles around, constantly weeding out those who were not up to the job of being the top team in the county.

There is nothing wrong with elitism. Sport is at its core an elitist business, it has to be. To win you have to be better than your opponent. Or at least in the case of Chelsea have more money. And the bloke was very good at certain aspects of management: he had imaginative training drills, good tactics and a keen awareness of issues such as hydration and diet. His problem was just that his desire to win made him completely blind to the sensitivities of some of his players. He concentrated his entire effort on a golden circle of half a dozen talented boys at the core of the squad, and almost completely ignored the rest. Which, when dealing with nine- and ten-year-olds hardly constitutes sensible psychology.

Hugo survived for a season under this stewardship, the occasional flourish of skill enough to persuade the coach that there must be something there worth persevering with. In a way, watching how things were unfolding and seeing that the standard was rising to the point of almost matching the local league clubs' academies, it would have been better to leave at the end of his first year, perhaps find somewhere less intense for the boy to go and just play football. But – and this was my fault – we never had that discussion. I just signed him up for the next season, telling him it was a good life lesson. Keep trying and things will happen, I said. There is a reward for effort, I said. Make the most of your opportunities, I said. The chances are bound to come your way. All you have to do is grab them.

The problem was, the chances didn't come his way. As things unfolded the following season, every week he would turn up to play, every week he would be made substitute and every week he would remain unused, left standing on the touchline, without so much as a kick. I would turn up to watch and would wait by the changing rooms as the coach went through his interminable pre-match talks, hoping that, when the team trotted out, the boy would be among them. Every week I would look down the line, counting off the players, one, three, five, eight . . . nine . . . ten . . . bollocks. Every week he would shuffle out at the back of the group, still in his tracksuit, his step getting wearier by the match.

As the perennial substitute, the coach would give him little tasks to do, ostensibly to keep him involved: 'Hugo, collect the practice balls'; 'Hugo, fill the water bottles after half-time'; 'Hugo, get a pen from the changing rooms to fill in the match card.'

Never the most organised of kids, he showed little enthusiasm for such jobs and often messed them up.

'Honestly, Hugo, can't you do anything properly?' he would be asked as he came back empty-handed from a task or after putting the wrong-coloured bibs in the wrong bag. The tone was joshing, but the meaning was clear. Everyone laughed and Hugo, like his father before him, became the team clown.

God, it hurt watching all this unfold. What I wanted was for him to succeed. Sure, in part that was to bask in his reflected glory, to have other parents come up and congratulate me on the boy's performance. But mostly it was for his own sake. How I wanted those daydreams playing on a loop in his mental cinema to come gloriously true.

I hesitated from stepping in and saying anything to the coach, though. Much as you might like to, you can't live your children's lives for them, you can't fight their battles. This was his scrap. This was his challenge. He would, I kept telling myself, be all the stronger for it.

'Try a bit harder in training,' I'd say.

And he'd say: 'But I do try, Dad, I do try.'

'Well, then it'll come,' I'd say.

'Yeah,' he'd say.

But we both kind of sensed it wouldn't.

Eventually I could bear it no longer and intervened. I collared the coach after a training session. Here I was, everything I told myself not to be, the pushy parent personified.

'Is there any chance he might get some game time?' I said. 'The thing is, he'll never improve if he doesn't play in matches. It's a vicious circle, because he doesn't play, he's dropping behind the other lads, so he's not going to win a place.'

'Well, you see,' said the coach, 'it's a tough league. We need our best players out on the pitch. And Hugo doesn't exactly help himself, does he?'

'What do you mean?'

'Well, he's on another planet most of the time. I mean, I asked him to fill the water bottles last week and he didn't put the tops back on properly, so everyone got soaked when they had a drink at half-time.'

Inside I was thinking, He wants to play football, not be your bloody skivvy. But I didn't say anything more than:

'Yeah, right, well, he can be like that.'

'Tell you what,' he said. 'Two weeks' time we've got an easy game. If things go all right, I'll start him in that. Not promising anything, but I'll do my best.'

As it happened, the weekend of that game, I was away working and my wife said she'd take him along. But she told me there didn't seem to be much point as he never seemed to get a game. I said I had the coach's word that he would get his chance. This could be the turning point, I said to her. Show commitment now and things could really improve, I said to him.

But there was no place in the starting line-up. Worried that another team was closing in on his position at the top of the table, against this weaker opposition the coach decided to play his strongest team, to build up the goal difference. For Hugo, it meant it was the fifth successive match in which he was a non-playing substitute. Five games on the trot he had not got a kick. On the way back from the game, alone in his mother's company, it all came out. He burst into tears; big gulps of misery.

'I hate it, hate it, hate it,' he said. 'Can I give up?'

'Of course you can,' she said, holding back a tear herself.

'Just don't tell Dad,' he said.

But she did tell me. And, afterwards, I sought him out in his bedroom, where he sat on the bed big-eyed as if waiting for a telling-off.

'Hey,' I said. 'If you want to give up I understand. I don't blame you.'

He looked at me as if a huge burden had been lifted.

'I thought you'd go mad,' he said. 'I only carried on because I thought you wanted me to.'

He was just ten years old.

A year or so later, he tried again, this time at another club. At first things went well. The coach was a cheery character, kindness itself. And Hugo got off to a cracking start, playing really well in a tournament, scoring the goal which took the lads to the semi-final. The level was not as high as he played at before, but at least here, I thought, he can enjoy his football again.

But soon things began to deteriorate. This most talkative of boys started to come home from training and say nothing. When asked how he had got on, it was always just 'all right'. Soon he was reluctant to go to sessions at all; I had to push him out the door. As for matches, on one occasion he told me the wrong rendezvous time for an away game. When we turned up, there was no one there; the game had been and gone. I blamed his woeful personal organisation and bollocked him accordingly. The next week I made sure he was there by ringing up the coach to find out when the game was taking place. I got him there on time and thought, Oh well, if I have to do that every week, it's not that much of a chore. But then, standing there on the side as the game unfolded, I witnessed something that made me shudder.

Morale was not good in the side. There was an

atmosphere of bickering rather than encouragement, with the more vociferous of the players constantly moaning. They just weren't a particularly cheery bunch.

But even so, what I heard that morning shocked me. When Hugo trotted on as substitute one of the boys shouted out, 'Oh God, not him.' Another one said: 'Well, we'll definitely lose now he's on.'

The thing was, Hugo looked in really good shape that day. He ran and chased and harried and made real effort. He was doing his best to adhere to my reasoning: if you make the commitment the reward will follow. But still it didn't. He got very little of the ball, even when he was in good positions and calling for it, it never seemed to come his way. At the end of the game, the goalkeeper ostentatiously came over to him and said, 'Well played, Hugo mate, you did really well.' But I noticed the one who had complained when the substitution was made scowling at the pair of them.

Later, when we were alone, I asked him what all that was about. How come that boy was so hostile? And why did nobody pass to him? He just said everything was fine. Clearly, though, something was happening, something was not right. So I persisted.

'Is everything OK?'

'Yeah.'

'But are you enjoying it?'

'It's fine, Dad, honestly.'

The next week, it happened again. This time, I was standing no more than five yards away, so there was no mistaking the intent. During the warm-up, as the boys jogged along the side of the pitch, one of the two who had sneered at Hugo the previous week started running along behind him, doing a mocking impression of his gait. There was nothing jokey or friendly about it. This wasn't banter.

He happened to score that game, twice in fact, but the two made no attempt to congratulate him. In fact, when the goalie ran out of his area to go over and ruffle Hugo's hair after his second, one of them shouted:

'What the hell are you doing? Get back in your goal, you twat.'

And I thought, Oh God.

'Come on, mate,' I said when he emerged from the changing rooms. 'What is going on?'

'Nothing,' he said. 'Honestly, nothing.'

But this time there were tears in his eyes.

It took another two weeks before the truth came out. As I suspected, he was being bullied by two of the team. It seemed this pair prided themselves on getting rid of any newcomers. They had, I learned subsequently, seen off three others over the previous season or so. Hugo went to a different school and that was sufficient cause to make him the next target. From the moment he arrived, he suffered from a continuous campaign of low-grade unpleasantness from these two. Most of it was verbal, but once at training, he told me several years later, they had given him the most painful wedgie of his life, hooking him up in the branch of a tree by his underpants. They bullied the other members of the team into ostracising him. Some joined in, others were more reluctant. The keeper in particular had stood out against them, going out of his way to support him. But it was clearly hurting the boy.

And once again, he kept his distress quiet, fearful that I would label him a quitter.

'But doesn't the coach do something?' I said.

'They only do it when he's not looking,' he said.

'So do you want to pack it in?' I said.

'Well . . . I . . . Yeah. Sorry.'

I rang the coach that evening and told him Hugo was leaving the team because of bullying. I filled him in with all the details. He seemed wearied by what I said, but not overly surprised.

'I sensed there was an undercurrent,' he said. 'But I'd kind of held off doing something. I'm sorry, I should have acted.'

I told him that it appeared they had concealed their actions from him, so there was no reason for him to feel bad. But he obviously did. A few weeks later, after Hugo had left, I heard that there had been a mighty rumble at training. The bullying issue bubbled to the surface when one of those responsible bitterly complained to the coach that there were no good players in the team and that's why they always lost. The coach lost his temper, shouting at them that they always saw off anyone new. The row that ensued was so intense, so bitter, the coach folded the team on the spot.

They reformed a few years later, at the under-eighteen level, without the principal bully. I'd bump into the goalie occasionally on Sunday mornings at various playing fields round the county and he always said to me, get Hugo to come along, we could use him. However, by now the lad was showing real flair for his new sport of choice – the Sunday-morning lie-in. These days, his skills are only occasionally unfurled in pick-up games in the park.

Poor Hugo, he had the misfortune to be our family's pioneer through boys' football. He was the guinea pig. I was convinced football would be good for him. Yet maybe organised sport wasn't the benevolent moral force I had fondly imagined. Maybe the life lessons it taught were unnecessary and harmful. Maybe I was just plain wrong.

But oddly, what I saw didn't put me off getting Barney involved. It wasn't the sport, I told myself, that had disappointed Hugo, it was the way it was practised. As I picked over the aftermath of Hugo's experience, I thought that things didn't have to be like that if the manager was on top of it. Yes, I thought I could do better. And I vowed if ever I was in charge of a bunch of lads, nobody would find themselves treated like he was. It was a promise that was subsequently to be tested to the limit.

So that's why I'm here today, standing on the touchline watching another defeat unfold. As the opposition's centre forward bears down on our defence time and again, I run through my mind what I could be doing with my Sunday morning if I had kept my mouth shut that day Doug asked for volunteers. I could be buying a new washing machine on a trip to Currys or nailing some trellising to the garden fence up which I might train some roses, or dead-heading said roses, or writing three overdue articles, or assaulting the pile of junk that is my office, or doing some weeding at the allotment, or watching self-important sportswriters dissecting the week's football on *Jimmy Hill's Sunday Supplement.*

Put that way, watching your boys, even as they face another demolition, suddenly doesn't seem that bad an option. Particularly as the determination even in defeat that some of them show makes the heart sing. Tim in particular is a titan, flinging himself into tackles, charging upfield with the ball, exhorting his team-mates with a constant 'C'mon Northmeadow.' He is rising to the challenge presented by a genuinely good team. Their centre forward is as fine a young player as I have seen: strong, skilful, brave, effortful, a real force. And you can't miss him, with a plume of vibrant red hair, he could play in the dark and illuminate the game. Afterwards, I ask their coach how he keeps this lad secret from the local league club. I'd have thought he had every quality needed to make it as a pro, I say.

'They haven't got any money for decent scouts,' he says. 'The only way they'll send someone down to look at a boy is if you ring them up and tell them. And guess what? I'm not going to tell them.'

Then I say to our lads not to worry. It might have been 4-0, I say, but it was no humiliation. I tell them that if they all play like Tim, they'll be fine.

'Put in the effort and the rewards will come,' I say.

But even as I walk away, I think maybe I should get myself a new script. Because this one just doesn't seem to work.

4

Go out and enjoy yourselves

Sometimes it feels as if my whole life is consumed by Northmeadow Under-Fourteens: waking hours, sleeping hours, the daydreams in between. Sometimes my head is so full of stuff like whether Luke would be better off at full back or on the wing and where on earth is this hole in which Barry says I should play Gio, that it seems physiologically impossible that there can be any space in my brain left for anything else. In fact, I do have a job. The good news is, it is one I can occasionally manipulate to serve the Northmeadow cause. When I became coach of Barney's team, I was writing sports interviews for a newspaper. Every week I was meeting people who knew how to do sport. I thought, Here's an opportunity. I reckoned they might have some tips a bit more useful than 'Get stuck in' or 'Clear it.' At the end of interviews, I used to ask my subjects: what one bit of advice would you give me for coaching young players? It didn't matter if they were footballers or rowers, an athlete or a jockey, they were bound to have something useful to suggest about motivation and preparation. They always responded, too, happy to chat about anything that wasn't the soap opera of their careers.

The habit has continued even after I left that job. Every time I meet someone who might be able to help, I ask. The advice has been varied and plentiful. Some have told me to let the ball do the work.

'Let the ball do the work,' said José Mourinho. 'Every exercise should have ball play. Fitness, everything, with ball. You play with ball, so why not train with ball?'

Others have talked me through little psychological ploys designed to boost team spirit.

'Giving everyone names in the five-a-sides is a great way to keep things buoyant,' said Big Ron Atkinson. 'That's where Sparky came from for Mark Hughes, a five-a-side nickname. Make sure that you reserve the best name for yourself, mind. I was always Pelé.'

Others, meanwhile, have produced a mini-masterclass in cliché.

'Just tell them this,' said one veteran knight of the realm who shall remain nameless. 'Lads, go out and enjoy yourselves.'

Actually that's a little unfair on Bobby Robson (oops). Almost all of those I have met told me that the biggest priority for any coach is to make sure everyone is having fun. Especially at our level, where we are engaged in a leisure activity, not moulding the professionals of the future. As Frank Dick, the former chief coach of UK athletics put it: never in the history of sport has anyone improved by being made to feel miserable. Everyone feels better about themselves when you tell them they have done well. Inevitably Clive Woodward had a little aphorism for it: encouragement pays dividends, he said. Advice I had clearly forgotten after we had been mauled 6-1 the other week.

Easily the most immediately effective tip I ever got,
however, did not come from a sportsman, it came from
a shrink. Willi Railo is renowned throughout Scandinavia
and much of Europe as a sports psychologist. His ability
to manipulate the sporting mindset has helped the careers
of golfers, distance runners and tennis players. More pertinent to football followers in England, though, is that he
can lay claim to the most dubious honour in world sport:
he is Sven-Göran Eriksson's mentor. This was the man
who helped Sven forge his coaching philosophy. He was
there alongside him as the old chancer progressed up the
managerial ladder from Sweden to Italy and then on to
Lancaster Gate, via the paying-in counter of the local
branch of NatWest. He was the one who gave Sven his
ideas.

These days, the only purpose in seeking out the bloke
responsible for Sven's career would be to chuck a bucket
of cold water over his head. But, hard though it is to believe,
given what has happened subsequently, when I went to
Norway in search of Railo back in 2001, Sven was regarded
as the smartest thing in football. We watched the Swede
on the touchline when England beat Germany in Munich
and we thought, This must be the way. What a harsh light
Sven cast over his predecessor, Kevin Keegan. How absurd
and old-fashioned was the badger-haired has-been's
coaching by comparison. There he was, prancing about
clutching his heart in an attempt to encourage his team to
perform better and yet he'd picked Gareth Southgate in
central midfield. Sven, on the other hand, seemed to us in
those days to ooze tactical sophistication. While Keegan
was flappy, overwrought and naive, Sven was cool, he was
objective, he was calm. As we watched his England perform
it seemed to us this studious, dome-headed Scandinavian

had unlocked the secret to coaching football. And the story went that it was Railo who had provided him with the key.

Railo, though, was a busy man and agreed to talk only if I came to see him where he was working, in Norway. I took Ryanair to Oslo and arrived in good time. Outside the airport, there was a minibus waiting with a sign on the front saying, 'Oslo city centre'. I boarded it and looked out of the window as the pines rolled by. After about fifteen minutes of driving, we headed on to a motorway. I assumed it must be the city's ring road. But the first road sign we passed read: 'Oslo 110 km'. Ryanair's definition of Oslo was clearly flexible, a bit like calling Birmingham London.

Nearly three hours later, I found Railo sitting at a table in a by-now empty restaurant, as the waiters finished clearing up the lunch things round him. It was obvious from the moment I saw him that Railo's active participation in sport was but a distant memory. His hair was an unruly busby and he wore a venerable tweed jacket, scuffed at the cuffs. There were ink stains on his shirt; he might easily have been mistaken for a mad professor. Especially when he grabbed me by the wrist and led me outside.

'We have no time to waste,' he said, sounding unnervingly like Ralph Fiennes's death-camp commandant in *Schindler's List*. 'You will follow me, yes?'

And off we went, out the back of the hotel and along an icy path to the bottom of what was unmistakably a ski-jump tower.

'We go up, yes?' he said in a voice that suggested this was not a discussion. We took a lift and arrived at the top of the scariest sporting venue I have ever been in. Here is where the cream of Europe's mountain youth spend their weekends, strapping a pair of planks to their feet and hurtling off into the gloaming at 90 mph, flying through the air for more than half a kilometre, the g-force peeling their cheeks back towards their ears. I peered out of the little glass lookout point at the summit and the whole of Oslo was laid out beneath us. What seemed about three miles below our feet lay the landing arena, its sides steepling up into terraces, which on jump days would be filled with voyeurs hoping for a cataclysmic tumble. Running from the top was the narrow scaffolding jump track itself, wobbling in a wind that seemed to be howling in direct from Siberia. Blimey, I thought, I should never have laughed at Eddie the Eagle. Even to attempt to jump off something like this, the man must have had a heart the size of a satellite dish.

Railo pulled open a door and ushered me outside. We stood at the top of the jump, our knees bent against the height, the pair of us clutching the safety rail with both hands. Looking down its vertiginous run, my stomach made a bold bid to escape through the soles of my feet.

'Dear God,' I said. 'What the hell would the sports psychologist say to somebody who was about to jump off here?'

'I would tell them this,' said Railo, peering gingerly down the launch pad. 'If you had half a brain you would just turn round and go straight back down in the lift.'

He then roared with laughter, grabbed me by the wrist again and pulled me back inside before the urge to leap became irresistible.

'Good,' he said shutting the door. 'We had to get that over with to see if you were serious.'

What, so this was a test of my resolve?

'Yes. Now we talk. So here is what you need to know.'

And off he went, his scattergun conversation taking in everything from the physical contents of the brain to the physiology of the bladder. Occasionally his stream of consciousness would peter out and he would go silent. At first I thought his head had imploded. But as he ignored my enquiries as to whether he was all right, I realised he was merely drawing breath before the next verbal assault. Eventually, after a two-hour lecture conducted in the hut at the top of a ski-jump tower, I managed to interrupt long enough to ask him for one practical piece of advice that might help my lads win a tournament they were taking part in the following weekend.

He went silent again. Then, after what seemed an age, he pronounced thus:

'Sit them down on the grass in a circle and tell them to shut their eyes, yes? Calmly, in a gentle voice, ask them to imagine touching the trophy. Then ask them to think through what they will do personally to help the team win. Tell them to imagine scoring the winning goal or saving the vital penalty or making a great tackle, yes? Ask them to think how they will feel if someone else goes home with that trophy and not them. Then when you are ready to go, tell them to open their eyes and to get out there and do what they have just imagined. I guarantee you it will work.'

A few days after our meeting I got the chance to try it out. The tournament was a six-a-side event in a market town about ten miles south of where we live. We had entered two teams in the under-nine section, with Jeff my co-manager back then looking after one and me the other. Jeff's team was soon knocked out and he decided to head home rather than watch our side's progress.

'Face it, this is a waste of time,' were his parting words. 'You're not going to win with this lot. We need to get rid of them and get some hard lads in from the estate. These are all wimps.'

It was a point of view. But this time Jeff was wrong. Largely driven by Lee who, at just eight years old possessed the most extraordinary will to win, we progressed through the early rounds to an epic semi-final victory. At the final whistle, the whole opposition team, their coach and many of their supporters burst into tears. It was, one of their red-eyed parents told me later, the first time they had ever lost.

There was no more than a ten-minute gap between the semi and the final and I watched the coach of our opponents fill it by geeing his boys up, making them sprint across the pitch, then lecturing them, insisting that they squeeze out every last drop. Though he didn't specify of what. He gave it the full Churchill number. I heard the words 'Get stuck in' used several times.

Meanwhile, I applied the Railo method. As instructed I sat the lads down in a circle, told them to shut their eyes and imagine wrapping their hands around the trophy. I could see one of the parents of the opposition spot us and nudge his mate to have a look at the bleedin' hippies sitting there all cross-legged and contemplative and out of it. I told the boys to determine in their own minds what they could do to ensure they won. I insisted they kept their eyes shut until I saw the referee walk out on to the pitch, the match ball under his arm. Then I told them to open up and go out and put into practice what they had imagined.

And you know what? They did just that. Their opponents, already exhausted by a long afternoon of football, had been finally, emotionally knackered by their coach's pre-match routine. Lee, playing with a poise that took the breath away, scored twice and set up a third for Gio. As the final whistle went, Gio's mum and I, the only two Northmeadow spectators in attendance, hugged each other like newly-weds. Barney and Fraser dashed off to the refreshment tent and bought half a dozen cans of pop which, in lieu of champagne, they shook up and sprayed over their mates, leaving a slick of sticky gloop on every item of clothing within a radius of ten feet. As they went forward to get their medals, their faces swathed in triumph, I thought, This is easy.

Looking back on it now, the reason we won was because the opposition were dead on their feet and Lee played with the kind of vigour that had the watching scouts from league clubs on the phone to Barry that evening, salivating. He illuminated the pitch that day. Like he'd swallowed a box of light bulbs. It was circumstances not sorcery. Just one of those things. But at the time, as we drove home, Barney urgently ringing his mum to share the news, I genuinely believed that I was in possession of the secret. It seemed that Railo had let me in to some Masonic order of success. I thought, as we carried the little cup into the house, Barney holding one handle, me the other, that we'd need to build an extension to store all the medals he was bound to win. I thought this triumph lark was never going to stop.

That, as it turned out, was the only time it ever worked. In fact, to date it is the only trophy the team has won. Over the years the Railo method became less and less effective. At first I tried it out at every possible opportunity, hoping to reconjure that moment. I even used it at a mate's fortieth birthday football game to concentrate the minds of our bloated, pink-cheeked, swelling-bellied crew. It had no effect, though Simon the barrister did fall asleep, snoring gently through my spiel. The last time I used it was when the boys were in the semi-final of an under-thirteen competition.

'Right,' I said. 'Sit down in a circle and shut your eyes.'

Luke sat in the lotus position.

'What, you're going to get us to meditate?' he said.

'Sort of,' I said.

'No,' said Tim. 'What he's going to say is, "Imagine touching the trophy. Imagine being this close to it and seeing someone else going home with it."'

Bugger: that was exactly what I was going to say. Now I quickly had to change tack.

'No, lads, I just want you to relax, stay calm, prepare yourselves mentally. Just shut your eyes and tell me what you can see.'

'I can see a slapper with big tits.'

There was much laughter. They bought this stuff when they were eight; twelve was something else altogether.

I ploughed on, telling them to keep their eyes shut and their lips sealed. But there was no way back when Luke ostentatiously keeled over and lay there with his legs and arms in the air like a dead cow. Barney almost wet himself at that.

Besides, the Railo method as practised by his leading disciple was soon to be discredited. Sven was a proven public failure and we coaches were looking elsewhere for inspiration. And for me that came, quite by chance, a week or so after the debacle against the giants who mullahed us 6-1. I was invited by the sponsors to watch England play against Spain in Madrid, the day Shaun Wright-Phillips was given verbals by the Bernabeu racists. At a lunch before the game, I found myself sitting next to Eric

Harrison. For coaches of youth football, this is the place-setting equivalent of being positioned next to the Dalai Lama: you are in close proximity to the man with all the answers. In charge of Manchester United's youth set-up for nearly twenty years, he was responsible for kick-starting the careers of the following: Norman Whiteside, Mark Hughes, Clayton Blackmore, David Platt, Ryan Giggs, Nicky Butt, David Beckham, Paul Scholes, Gary Neville, Phil Neville, Wes Brown, Kieran Richardson, John O'Shea and Giuseppe Rossi. Plus Robbie Savage, but then nobody's perfect.

If you speak to any of his charges, they make it sound like Harrison was a training-ground tartar, a ferocious taskmaster whose after-match bollockings threatened changing-room paintwork across the country. According to Blackmore, Harrison's temper was the most terrifying thing he has encountered in nearly thirty years in football. Billy Garton, a centre back who played a dozen games for the United first team before succumbing to ME, recalls crying himself to sleep the evening after a humiliating dressing-down in front of the rest of the lads. And Ryan Giggs says that after being brought up on Harrison's tirades, Alex Ferguson's hairdryer seemed but a cooling breeze. Yet it was hard to reconcile that ferocious reputation with the kindly, attentive man passing me the paella. When I finally plucked up the courage to ask my inevitable question, he turned and looked at me.

'You're coaching a bunch of under-fourteens?' he said. 'Best job in the world.'

We then talked for a couple of hours, through the main course, past the pudding, over the coffee. Much of the time was taken up by lengthy perorations on the joy that is Paul Scholes.

'He was the best of the lot, Scholesy,' he said. 'I knew from the moment I first clapped eyes on him as a nine-year-old. You want to know the one thing that is cast-iron guaranteed to turn your lads into winners? Get a young Paul Scholes on your team.'

Sadly, unless Luke turns ginger overnight, that is unlikely to happen.

But Harrison had more to say. The advice poured out: on psychology, on training methods, on physiology. His ideas were an amazing mixture of the simple and the inspired, bereft of jargon, stripped of psychobabble, just endless good sense. He suggested, for instance, that it was an idea to train on a surface, such as a tennis court, marked with straight lines.

'Get the lads into pairs and have them passing along the lines. Amazing how much it helps.'

It does too. I've tried it and it works.

He also told me of a trick he came up with after watching an advert for road safety on the television. It was his version of the green cross code.

'Get them to look right and left before they receive the ball,' he said. 'Just a quick glance in each direction. Helps them take in everything around them. Get them into that habit and it will improve them as a player by 25 per cent. We used to do that all the time. Ooh, they hated me when I went on and on about it. Even in five-a-sides, I'd stop the game and give a free-kick to the opposition if someone didn't look right and left before they took a pass. But they got the hang of it eventually. You watch Scholesy now. He still does it.'

A couple of weeks later, I was at a game at Old Trafford and made a point of studying the great United midfielder. Harrison was right. Scholes did indeed still do it, his head flicking quickly either side to assess how much space he had the moment he received the ball. It was part of the reason he could pick his way through the gridlock of midfield as if he had a sat-nav system embedded in his forehead.

I tried out the Harrison idea at the next possible opportunity.

'Right,' I said. 'Here's an easy drill. Pass the ball to each other, but the man receiving it has to look right and then left before he traps it.'

You would have thought, judging by their reaction, I had just asked the lads to complete a quantum physics equation. It confused them horribly. The training pitch was filled with boys looking right, left, centre, anywhere but at the ball. If they didn't follow the ball's path along the ground all the way on to their toes, they simply did not seem to know where it was. To give them their due, they tried. Yet even Ryan, the most studious of trainers, couldn't get the hang of it. Luke drove himself giddy in the attempt, flicking his head madly from side to side. At one point, so extreme were his head movements, he had actually fallen over before the ball came anywhere near him.

'Everyone,' I said, as Luke picked himself up from the tarmac. 'This is the drill that made Paul Scholes the player he is today. Let's get it right.'

Fat chance: it was over the moment I laughed as Luke ran round the tennis court shaking his head like a heavy metal fan at a Metallica gig. From then on, everyone was fabricating comedy pratfalls. I told them they would have to keep at it until they mastered it. For three weeks we tried. For three weeks the result was mayhem. Plus in Luke's case a cricked neck. Eventually, on the way home after yet another failure, Barney told me it was best to drop it. It was never going to work, he reckoned.

'Face it, Dad,' he said. 'None of us is ever going to be Paul Scholes.'

5

The pleasures of victory

Who needs Paul Scholes anyway, eh? Even if it is a lucky one against a team with only ten men because one of the parents' cars has a flat tyre on the way over and their centre back and captain never make it to the ground, a win is still a win. Today we won our first match in the A League. We are now officially a bunch of winners. That is what I tell the boys after the game.

'Ten men still have to be beaten,' I say. 'You've shown you can live in the best company. We're on the march.'

The thing is, I tell Barry afterwards, as long as we finish above two teams in the league, we're bound to stay up. Happy days are here. It suddenly all seems so simple.

'Oh, you won, then?' says Ellie as we walk in through the front door, grinning. 'Who were you playing? Snow White and the Seven Dwarfs?'

I can brush aside her wit. I am officially happy: the boys tried their hardest and got due reward. Cause and effect. This is surely what it is all about.

My cheeriness does not last long. As I arrive at the training session the week following our win, Tim fills me in.

'Heard the news?' he says. 'There's a rumour Bamfield have folded. All their results will be null and void.'

'Nah,' I say. 'Can't be true. They can't have. The league table was in the paper at the weekend. We had three points. It was there in black and white.'

'Check out the league website,' says Tim, who spends much of his spare time on the site's discussion forum. 'Everyone's saying they've folded.'

As soon as I get home, I'm on the computer. He is right. It is there in the news section. 'Bamfield Under-Fourteens Fold,' reads the headline, 'click on link below for full details.'

A couple of months into the new season, the manager and players of Bamfield could see no future other than extended humiliation and have packed it in. Apparently losing to us was the final straw: the decision to give up had been taken on the way home from that defeat.

It happens all the time in boys' football. In Barney's age group alone, ten teams have given up since we started. In the early days, the league ran to three divisions and there was a waiting list to get in. If it goes on like this for much longer, soon there will be just the one.

Holding a side together when they start losing is not easy. Especially as boys get older. Once the hormones kick in, they are tempted away by the siren call of Sunday-morning lie-ins. As teenage starts to impinge, so hanging around outside HMV or spending the afternoon huddled for three hours round a shared latte in Starbucks with fourteen of your friends suddenly seems a more tempting lifestyle option than running around a field forlornly chasing a lost cause. The vicious cycle locks in as good players of a failing side are lured away by schoolmates to better clubs. Managers, unable to motivate themselves, never mind their players, eventually decide it is less grief to admit defeat and walk away than to attempt to battle on. The result is that over a hundred kids of Barney's age in our area have stopped playing football altogether. It must be assumed from the stomachs congregating outside McDonald's on a Saturday afternoon that many of them now do no exercise whatsoever.

Clearly, Bamfield have decided things can only get worse. Though their coach has ensured that for his own son things are about to get significantly better; he has given him the chance to enjoy a bit of success for a change by the simple expedient of signing the boy up for Kington Juniors, the side that has won the league every year it has been in operation. A couple of days after Tim breaks the news, a posting on the website reveals that any points accumulated against Bamfield do not count. The consequence is, we are in a suddenly much tougher league. And we still do not have a win to our name. Or as my wife puts it rather succinctly: we are altogether pointless.

6

The chairman

Even as I am speaking I have a voice in my head issuing clear, precise, unmistakable instructions:

'Just say no,' it is saying. 'You know what he wants. Just say you can't do it. You haven't got the time. Say no. That's all you have to do. No one will accuse you of not doing your bit. It's a simple word. No, no, no, no, no. No.'

But my mouth isn't listening. Instead this is what comes out of it:

'Sure. Yeah, no, definitely. Let's meet up. When's good for you?'

I'm speaking to Ian on the phone. He is a new arrival on the club committee. Since Doug has been unavailable following an operation, he has been running things. Together with Malcolm, the manager of one of the younger age groups, he has set about transforming the administration with an admirable gale of energy, bombarding us all with ideas and emails, knocking us out of our inertia, challenging our complacency. He wants to professionalise things, he says. And he wants to meet up and buy me a beer as soon as possible. He has an idea, he says, which he wants to run by me. I can tell by the tone of his voice what it is he wants me to do. He wants me to be the club chairman. I do not want to be club chairman. I am a hopeless administrator. I hate bureaucracy. I get no kick from meetings. So all I need to do is to say no.

The thing is, I know what it takes to run a boys' football club, what it takes to be chairman. Because I've seen Doug in action. For years, certainly as long as I have been around, Doug has been in charge. He sorted things. He did things. It was his club. Sure, we had a committee made up of the team managers of each group, plus Wilko, the fixtures secretary, who kept details of all forthcoming games in a big book filled with impenetrable grids compiled in a code no one would even dare try to decipher. But it was Doug who did all the rest.

This was how committee meetings would go in Doug's day. He would book the local Conservative club and a few of us would reluctantly head along, pulling the collars of our coats up as we walked through the door; not against the chill, but lest anyone we know saw us entering the building. People nearby must have wondered who we were, all these blokes going into the Tory club with coats on and their collars pulled up in the middle of May. Once inside, we would gather round a table in the room next to the indoor bowling alley where the Aunt Sally club was meeting. To the rhythmic clack of wooden balls against wooden pegs we'd begin with the secretary's report. Since nobody had stepped forward to fill the vacant position of club secretary, Doug was acting as secretary.

'Not much to report, gentlemen,' he would say, 'just the usual.'

Happy that this was a true and accurate minute of the

proceedings, the chairman (Doug) would move things on quickly to the treasurer's report. Since the treasurer was also an unfilled place in the committee structure at the moment, Doug was in sole charge of club funds and would tell us that there was:

'Not much to report here either, gentlemen, the usual really.'

Then, after the subscriptions secretary (Doug) and the boys' league liaison officer (Doug) and the overseas tour coordinator (Doug) had informed us that there was not much to report, the chairman (Doug) would proceed to any other business. Occasionally someone who had not been lulled into a gentle sleep by the strangely soothing soundtrack of clacking balls and Doug's hacking cough, would raise an issue. Perhaps it would be the lack of keys to the clubhouse door, or the poor state of the changing rooms, or the drifts of dog mess now threatening to turn the lower pitch brown. Then, after we had chatted about it for a few minutes, Doug would say:

'OK, gentlemen, leave it to me.'

At which everyone would think, That's a result, he didn't ask me to do anything. Then the chairman would declare the meeting closed, set a date for the next one and we'd pull up the collars on our coats and make a dash for our cars, hoping we had got away once more without being seen leaving the building.

All that subterfuge, all that clandestine collar-lifting, though, seemed pretty pointless. There really wasn't much need to have a committee as Doug did everything for the club. He paid the bills, he organised the five-a-side tournament, he arranged the annual tour to Holland, he bought the kit, he supplied the balls, he ironed the club name on to the back of tracksuits he had bought as a cheap job lot, he stepped in when there wasn't a coach for an age group, he persuaded parents to become team managers, he had the spare keys to the clubhouse and he yelled at any local resident exercising their dogs out on the field to bloody well clear it up. Thinking back, I can't remember anyone doing anything else. If we had a raffle to raise funds, it was Doug who sorted it. When we needed to talk to the council about pitch markings, it was Doug who talked to the council about pitch markings. Or probably shouted at them. It was certainly Doug who, through his wholesale delivery business, supplied all the stock for the tea bar. And put his son Robert in charge of running it.

'I hate football,' Robert told my daughter one Sunday morning, as she bought some of his virulently coloured chewy sweets and E-numbers masquerading as a fizzy drink.

'So why are you here?' she said.

'Cos my dad's paying me.'

Yes, it was Doug's club all right: he even employed the staff.

Then, one committee meeting a couple of seasons back, Doug didn't show up. He was ill. The cough was getting worse. He was laid up in bed. It was then, in his absence, that Lester, the manager of the under-nines, shocked us all by proposing a serious motion. This wasn't about door keys or dog shit. It wasn't about the grass being too long on the seven-a-side pitch or the nutritional value of the stock in the tea bar. His idea was a pretty radical one: that we wind down Northmeadow altogether and amalgamate with the local Isthmian League club to become their feeder side. Let them sort out the admin, was his idea, and allow the managers to get on with coaching the boys. It would mean we could offer players the chance of football beyond the under-eighteen level, provide a path into the football pyramid. The non-league club was well up for it, he said. He was convinced that together we could become a huge thing in local football, second only to the big professional club. Of course, the Northmeadow name would disappear and we'd play in this club's colours, at their ground. But did that really matter if things were put on a sounder footing off the pitch?

I seem to remember at the time of the meeting no one really paid the idea much heed: it hadn't come from Doug, after all, so it didn't seem plausible or likely. It wasn't going to happen without the big man. After Lester had proposed it, we'd all just put our collars up as usual and made the dash for the anonymity of our cars. I thought nothing more of it and went back to worrying about formations and tactics for Sunday.

But when he heard, Doug went apoplectic. He called everyone from his sickbed. He was on the phone to me for two hours, during which I probably said three words.

'I want an extraordinary general meeting,' he wheezed, his cough rattling the phone wires. 'I won't let them destroy our club. I bloody won't let them. And you can come along and bloody vote against it.'

So, as soon as he was on his feet again, Doug called us all together for an extraordinary general meeting. He booked a room in a local pub, allowing even those who felt philosophically uncomfortable in the Conservative club to attend. As I pulled into the car park, he was getting out of his van.

'I hate bloody politics,' he said to me as we walked into the bar. 'It's a boys' football club, for Christ's sake. Why all this haggling and infighting? The trouble with me is, I just

don't know if I'll be able to keep my temper. I'll probably chin the bastard.'

It was a charged evening. For the first time I could
recall, everyone was interested in something beyond the
narrow horizons of their age group. Malcolm took the
chair because Doug felt he wanted to speak without
restraint. We all sensed what that might mean and hoped
the foundations of the pub were up to it.

Lester spoke first and outlined his thoughts. The gist
of his argument was that this was a good move for all
managers, because they didn't have to do any admin at
all. It would all be done for us.

'Let's face it, we're in a pretty ramshackle state here,'
he said. 'The clubhouse is falling down, the tea bar's
rubbish—'

'Hang on a bloody minute,' rasped Doug, standing up
out of his chair. 'I'll not have my tea bar insulted.'

'It's your tea bar that's an insult,' said Lester.

'Say that again outside,' said Doug, now leaning across
the table.

'Guys, guys, come on,' Malcolm said. 'One at a time.
Let's have a bit of order. Doug, let's hear Lester out.'

'Well, I won't bloody have my tea bar—'

'Doug.'

'The things is,' said Lester, after Doug had sat down,
grumbling and wheezing, and lit himself another cigarette
to settle his cough, 'we're not moving forward. The only
people who do anything committee-wise are team managers
and, naturally enough, they want to concentrate on their
teams. Which means nothing gets done, unless Doug does
it. And we're all grateful to him for what he does.'

'Yeah, bloody sounds like it,' grumbled Doug.

'My point is, it's just hand to mouth every year. We're

racing to stand still. What I'm saying is, this gives us a chance to face reality, stop stumbling on and go off somewhere where we'll be looked after. That's all I'll say: if we don't do this, we're going to die anyway.'

There was, when he finished, pandemonium as everyone tried to speak at once. Several committee members who had previously been assumed not to be in possession of vocal chords became very exercised. Everyone wanted a say. Barry, who had played for the first-ever Northmeadow team as a boy, fumed at the idea of us folding.

'It's not folding,' Lester said. 'It's trying to progress.'

'What, in the sense the dodo was trying to progress?' said Barry.

No one, though, was as unhappy as Doug.

Much to the evident surprise of many who wrongly characterised him as a joke, a Del Boy who used the club to wheel and deal and sell on his past-its-sell-by-date stock, he stood up and proceeded to give a brilliant speech: passionate, well-argued, to the point, directly addressing each of Lester's points. His belief was that the club was an entity of huge value that shouldn't be thrown away. It was a community asset. We should be proud of it, proud of what we'd done for the boys and proud of the future, too, proud to take it on.

'It's been going thirty years this club,' he said. 'It was started by two guys to give boys a game of organised football and now we run ten teams at all age groups. Bazz was here then as a kiddie and now he's helping to run his boy's team. You don't throw that sort of tradition away lightly. It's football, that's what it's about, giving kids something so that they're not hanging around street corners knocking our mums and dads over the head. If we can't do that now, thirty years on, if we're saying we can't be bothered to do a bit of admin to keep it going, then I'm sorry, gentlemen, I think that's shameful. An absolute disgrace. Me, I just want to say this: Long live Northmeadow Youth.'

There had been a moment or two's silence after that. During which you could almost see the thought spreading round the room; the thought that said, Hang on, this is quite a good thing we have here. Let's not dissolve the club, let's make it better. We had a vote and Lester's proposal was almost unanimously rejected. Actually, it might have been unanimous; I seem to recall Lester himself voted against it. Then a couple of people (I might have been one of them) said things could never develop if Doug had to do everything. It's not fair to keep making him do it all. So Ian and Malcolm had stepped forward and said they would help him, take some of the burden off his shoulders. As we left that night, Doug looked thrilled; he got back in his van wearing the smile of the vindicated.

Then, to no one's great surprise who had seen him over the years pacing the touchline, wheezing and gasping even as he drew on his fifteenth Lambert and Butler of the morning, who knew that in addition to running the club he was running his own delivery business, working eighteen hours a day and often just catching a couple of hours sleep in his van in a lay-by, Doug fell ill again. The cough took up full squatter's rights over his lungs. He needed an operation on his chest, and Lesley, his wife, told him he had to pack in the chairmanship otherwise it would kill him.

'Don't know why she's fussing,' he said to me. 'You've got to go sometime, haven't you? I'd have thought she'd be glad to see the back of me.'

But Lesley persisted. So, reluctantly, disappointedly and

as if he were giving up his baby for adoption, he had decided to let go, resign. We were standing on almost the same spot on the pitch where he had corralled me into being a team manager some five years earlier when he told me. There were tears steaming up his glasses as he spoke. And I thought, What the hell is going to happen to the club? It was like the canary had just died.

Now, nearly a year after he went, Ian and Malcolm want to have a drink. I can guess what they are going to say.

'Just say no,' my wife says as I leave the house to meet them.

'Just say no,' I tell myself as I walk along the street.

'Just say no,' the voice is still saying as I walk into the pub and spot the two of them sitting up by the bar.

But what I actually say, half an hour later after they have talked me through their plans, is:

'OK, I'll think about it.'

The thing is, Ian and Malcolm are very good salesmen.

'It's a purely ceremonial position,' says Ian. 'We just want you to use your experience to give us guidance. And maybe use your contacts to get us some big names in for the presentation evening.'

'What, you think I can get Fergie along to hand out the end-of-season medals?' I say, my voice, I assume, dripping with sarcasm.

'Brilliant. That would be terrific,' says Ian.

I gulp.

'But the thing is,' I say, 'Doug did everything.'

What I mean by this is pretty clear. Doug was the chairman and he did everything. If I become chairman, I don't want to do everything. I really don't want to be the bloke who everyone rings up when there's a problem.

If someone needs the gate key at nine on a Sunday morning, I don't want to be the person who has to drive up to the ground and give it to them. When some crackhead breaks into the clubhouse, I don't want to be the person who has to go up and sort out a list of what they nicked. When the residents complain about the 4×4s double-parking on their street on a Sunday morning, it is not my number I want them ringing. I'm just not cut out for that sort of thing. I can't administer anything. You should see the state of my office, I tell them.

Ian listens to my droning on and then says:

'It won't be like that. I give you my firm promise, administration won't be an issue. Malcolm and I will do all that. The chairmanship is purely ceremonial.'

'So why doesn't one of you two become the chairman?' I say.

'That's the whole point,' says Ian. 'We want to change the administrative ethos of the club. Put it on a more businesslike footing. You don't get the chairman of a blue chip company sorting out the finances or taking the minutes at board meetings. That's other people's jobs. Our jobs.'

'Purely ceremonial?' I say.

'Purely ceremonial,' they say.

'OK,' I say.

'Great,' they say.

And we shake hands, the new chairman and them.

'You idiot,' says my wife when I come home and tell her the news. 'You'll regret it.'

'But it's a purely ceremonial position,' I say. 'Like the mayor: wear the chain of office and hand out the prizes.'

'Bet you within six months you'll be going up at nine on a Saturday morning with the gate key.'

'Not going to happen.'
'It will. Guarantee it.'

This all happened last season. So far this year I have been up at the ground with a key three times. And only this morning a woman in the house abutting the seven-a-side pitch rang to tell me she had a broken pane in her green-house. What, she wanted to know, was I going to do about it?

7

The man in black

A couple of days ago, this posting appeared on the boys' league website discussion forum. It was written by someone signing themselves 'Tractor' (not, I assume, a town-dweller):

'There I go, turning up every week in the naive assumption that I'm going to ref a game of kids' football. I always end up cursing my own misfortune that I don't have a degree in human psychology or a working knowledge of adult mental health issues. Rule number one is that youth football is second only to Stella Artois in its ability to change adult behaviour for the worse.'

It was a good line, that, about the Stella. So good I thought I might nick it. And, with his suggestion that the man in the middle has become nothing more than a sponge to soak up the psychoses of the modern parent, Tractor had a point. Without the referee there can be no organised football for our children. Yet people seem to behave as if anxious to rid the game of his very presence at the earliest opportunity. They scream and bawl at some volunteer for the simple reason that he is not as capable as the guys they see on telly.

The tales of woe involving refs at kids' matches are everywhere. A mate of mine tells of seeing a dad run out on to the pitch to attack the official with a beer bottle. Another witnessed a pitch invasion in which the ref was chased into the car park, where he jumped into his motor and sped off, leaving his clothes, shoes, bag, everything behind in the dressing room. A linesman was beaten up in our league only last season, kicked to the ground by three players and a parent for the crime of flagging an equalising goal offside. Things are getting so bad, people say to me, that it won't be long before we start behaving like Americans. Didn't you read that story in the papers, they say, the one about the parent in Chicago who grabbed hold of the referee after his son's ice hockey team had lost and bashed his head repeatedly on the ice, killing him?

We can all agree what's gone wrong. The trouble is a lack of respect has seeped down from the top. Boys' team managers behave like they're in the Premiership, aping what they see of José and Arsène and Big Sam on *Match of the Day*, with their whinges and their whines, forgetting that the bloke who turns up on a Sunday morning isn't on a sizeable salary like Graham Poll. He's just giving up his time for a bit of beer money (enough for about four pints, usually). No wonder refs are disappearing faster than the Amazonian rainforest. Who'd want to do it? Unless they are a certifiable masochist, that is.

The FA is trying to fight against the rising level of referee abuse. They advise all clubs to issue a charter that members and their parents have to sign. It is like the ones they have at Premiership academies, insisting on respect for the referee and acceptance of his judgement from both spectators and participants. Ian suggested we take up the charter as club policy last season: a wise idea. The ref is the lubricant that keeps the machinery of our game going. He deserves to be nurtured, not insulted.

But then, there is just one problem. One minor issue here. Given that the referee is an endangered species, given that he needs to be nurtured and respected, what do you do when you encounter the prat in black?

The first time I saw him in action was at a five-a-side tournament the season Barney's team started as under-eights. It was played on a scorching day in June, so hot the grass was turning to straw before your eyes. And the heat was hardly reduced by a set of rules that many of the participants, particularly the younger ones, found impossible to grasp.

The most difficult one involved the semi-circular goal-keeper's area. Only the goalies were allowed into it; if an attacker strayed across the white line, the defence was awarded a free-kick. But if a defender entered his own box, then a penalty was to be given. It was a tough punishment for little kids and most of the referees on duty were pragmatic in the way they applied the rule. If a boy ran into his own box to prevent a goal being scored, then they'd blow for a spot kick. But if a kid wandered accidentally into the area while play was up the other end, then they would ignore the infringement and just have a quiet word with the miscreant, suggesting he try not to do it again.

There was one referee that day, however, who liked nothing better than to parp on his whistle the second a toe crossed the line. Balding and bespectacled, his shorts spread tight across his substantial lower reaches, I had

watched him already give about five penalties before he
took charge of a game featuring our boys. When he waddled
on to the pitch, he was confronted by a chap playing for
the opposition who looked like his mini-me: A tubby little
Billy Bunter figure with the same bottle-bottomed glasses
and the same circulation-constricting kit. As the game
kicked off, I thought to myself: this lad might have difficulty coping with Lee's pace. Lee, though, was rendered a
bystander in what followed. Within about thirty seconds
of the kick-off, the little tubby had strolled, apparently
without a care in the world, a foot or two into his own
area. It was the most minor of transgressions, he clearly
wasn't interfering with play. In truth, this was the kind of
kid who could be on the pitch for days on end without
interfering with play. The referee, though, immediately blew
his whistle and marched to the spot, semaphoring like an
overexcited Italian traffic cop.

'Penalty,' he shouted. The kid looked nonplussed. And
remained where he was, a couple of feet inside the area
as Kal took a run-up from the halfway line and blammed
the ball as hard as he could in that subtle way eight-year-
olds do. It was a goal, but our lads barely celebrated; they
sensed this wasn't earned, it was soft. On the far touchline, I could see the fat lad's manager going bananas.

'You twat,' he shouted at the boy. 'That's your fault.
Now bloody sort yourself out.'

A couple of the boy's team-mates joined in the abuse.

'Yeah, you twat,' one of them said.

The kid stood there his bottom lip wobbling, his face
pinking up with the humiliation as the game kicked off
again. It became immediately clear that nobody had taken
a moment to explain exactly what it was that he had
done to earn such opprobrium. Instead of talking through

the rule with him, the manager just yelled at him that he
had let everybody down and that he should get his bloody
finger out. Nor had the referee thought it might be an
idea to point out what he had done. Nor, to my shame,
had I.

Which all meant, no more than two minutes later, that
the boy did it again. At the time the ref was up the other
end of the pitch. His manager, however, saw what he was
doing and bawled at him:

'Get out the bloody area.'

Instead of sounding a warning, this shout merely alerted
the referee. The man with the whistle turned round. And,
like Bunter spotted by the beak trying to clamber into
the tuck shop to stock up on illicit grub, there was the
lad, caught red-handed standing about three feet from his
goalkeeper, who looked a little alarmed at having sudden
company.

'Penalty,' announced the ref. He then marched forward,
unbuttoning his top pocket as he went and from within
it removed a yellow card.

'Second offence,' he said, standing over the poor kid
who stared up at the yellow card slack-mouthed with
misery. 'I have no alternative but to book you.'

What ensued was almost too painful to watch. Kal
dispatched the penalty and returned, rather sheepishly, to
his own half. With the ball lying in the corner of the
goal, the manager, the parents and the other players in
the fat lad's team shouted their complaints at him. As the
ignominy rained down, he stood and looked around him,
his mouth tight and small, just for a moment a little button
of defiance. Although made aware by all the yelling what
he had done – let his team-mates down, let his manager
down, let himself down – you could tell by his body

language he still had no idea how he had done it. He looked baffled, bemused, as if fate – unbidden – had simply chucked a bucket-load of stinking offal on his head. He still did not understand what he had done to break the rules so catastrophically. He'd merely walked across the pitch and now everyone was shouting at him as if he had just backed their prize Mercedes over a cliff. As he stood there, his manager's voice drifted across the pitch.

'You dickhead,' the man yelled. 'Look what you done. We're 2-0 down thanks to you. I hope you're pleased with yourself.'

Which was when the kid reached a point of decision in his head. For the first time in the game, he suddenly broke into a run and dashed off the pitch, past his manager and headed into a small copse just beyond the touchline. Here he climbed up a tree and sat in its branches for the remainder of the competition.

'Yeah, run off why don't you, you dickhead,' the manager shouted at him as he went. 'Good riddance. We're better off with four men.'

Never mind anyone else, watching that I almost burst into tears.

Nobody, it seemed to me, came out of that incident well. A small boy had been wretchedly abused and we were all culpable. His manager, his team-mates and their parents had behaved dreadfully. I felt guilty for days afterwards that I had not instructed Kal to do the Corinthian thing and miss the penalties. And why – if I could see he was having difficulties working things out – hadn't I walked on to the pitch and explained the rule to him?

But the person who had to take the major share of the blame was the ref. If he had simply stopped play and ensured the poor lad understood what was happening, everyone would have benefited. This wasn't the final of the Champions League. He didn't have an assessor from UEFA watching his every move to ensure he complied with the rule book. This was a preliminary round in a five-a-side tournament for eight-year-olds. The ref was simply wrong.

And guess what? Today he's back.

The opposition's supporters are parking up as I arrive. They are more people carrier than white van. There is a new Saab among their motors. And a BMW 4×4. As they get out of their cars and walk across the pitch, I notice one of the older supporters – a granddad perhaps – is wearing a Barbour. Won't be any touchline problems from this lot, then, I tell myself.

Which is just as well, as before we even kick off, the bad news starts to stack up like planes into Heathrow. Kal and Lee are injured, Paul is off doing some other sport and Luke is lost in a Bermuda Triangle of domestic arrangements that I am unable to follow from about the point where his dad tells me that, if they are to get to Birmingham on time to rendezvous with Luke's cousins, perhaps Luke could leave about 11.30.

'Richard, the game kicks off at 11.30.'

'Ah, right,' he says. 'Don't suppose there's much point him being there just for the warm-up?'

Then a bad day gets infinitely worse when I see emerging from the dressing room the man himself. It is not the official I had been expecting, the one stated on the league's email listing referees' appointments, the one who officiates with a smile on his face and sings in the dressing room. It may have been a couple of years ago and I haven't seen him since, but I recognise this one immediately. It's him all right. His kit, if anything, is even tighter than it was that day. On his black shirt are at least eleven embroidered badges, sewn like Cub Scout insignia, across his chest.

'Oh, it's you, is it?' is his opening line as he ignores my outstretched hand of welcome.

'Well, I hope we don't have any incidents like the last time we met.'

Ah, right, he remembers. I tell him I hope not too. I hope to God nothing like that ever happens again. It probably won't: Jeff's not here for a start.

'I'd be obliged if you could conduct a full check of the playing area for dog excreta.'

The creases on his shorts, I notice, are so sharply ironed they constitute a dangerous weapon.

'And I'd like to have a word with all the principals.'

'Principals?'

'Team officials, captains and volunteer referee's assistants, please.'

So when I introduce myself to their manager, I say: 'The ref wants a word before the game.'

'Yeah,' he says. 'We've already met. Mate of yours?'

Five minutes before the kick-off, just as I'm in the middle of my pre-match chat ('Above all, lads, make sure you track back'), the referee blows his whistle and indicates that we should join him in the centre circle. Tim, Barry and Franz's dad, Karl, who acts as our linesman, and I head over. When we arrive, the lecture begins.

'Referee's assistants: I expect you to be au fait with the latest interference laws, and your job is to signal immediately and clearly if an infringement is made. Managers: jewellery should be removed by all players, boys' socks must be pulled up to cover their shinguards and I will be making a full boot inspection before the game. Any boy with inappropriate studs will not be allowed to participate. And everyone, I will not tolerate foul language of any kind, but in particular blasphemy. Anything of that sort from any quarter, supporters and managers included, will warrant a caution and will be reported to the county FA. Please inform your players of my feelings on this issue.'

'Well,' their manager says to me as we walk away, 'your mate's a bundle of laughs.'

I know they are a good side. This is their first year in this competition; they won the league in the next-door district several times and have moved across hoping for a bit more of a challenge. We played them in the county cup a couple of seasons ago and did well to come away losing just 3-0. Rory, standing in as keeper that day, prevented a rout, as I recall. So I am not expecting much. Another day, another defeat.

And within two minutes of the kick-off, I know we are in for a game. Their midfielder puts in a hard tackle on Ryan that sends him scuttling to the turf. It is an uncompromising, muscular smack, a pertinent reminder that these are little boys no longer. For all its physicality, though, it looks fair to me. Ryan may now be on the ground, holding his ankle, but their player won the ball. The referee, however, not only blows for a foul, he calls the lad over for a lecture. The player is fuming.

'I got the ball, ref,' he says, both his arms outstretched, pointing at the object in question. He turns to his manager on the touchline and says: 'Tell him I got the bloody ball.'

Which is exactly what the manager does:

'Come on, ref, leave it out, he got the bloody ball.'

But the ref does not leave it out. He tells the player if he does that again, he will be booked. The lad, uncertain as to what it is that he has done that he should not do again, looks once more to his manager.

'Carry on, son,' the manager shouts. 'You've done nothing wrong.'

And thus is set the pattern of the game. At every challenge by them, the referee blows his whistle, and the opposition players appeal to their manager, who makes his feelings known. It becomes what sociologists call a pattern of repeat behaviour: the more they complain, the more the ref blows up. Within twenty minutes, the whole contingent of their supporters is shouting at his every decision, right or, usually, wrong. The manager is incandescent, his face a spreading vision of fury. By the time his centre back is booked for a late lunge on Adam, the man's complexion has turned the colour a bathroom designer would describe as terracotta.

'Jesus, ref.'

It is that, I think, that does it. Oozing pomposity, strutting across the pitch as if he is Pierluigi Collina after swallowing an overdose of pedantry pills, the ref marches over to the manager and, when he is standing directly in front of him, nose to nose, with a theatrical flourish, holds up a yellow card.

'I will not tolerate blasphemy,' he says. 'You cannot say you weren't warned.'

It is, you might think, an insanely brave thing to do. There he is, not a tall man, wearing glasses, his shorts so tight if he tried to run away he would soon exhaust all the blood supply in his legs, surrounded by a group of supporters who have lost control of their temper. If this

were an ice hockey game, if this were Chicago, his head
would already be bouncing on the ice. I reckon at any
moment I will have to run across the pitch and interrupt
a lynching. I conduct a quick audit of who might back
me up. Apart from Barry, I can't see any of our lot being
too keen. Hamish, Alan, Richard, James, Derek: all the
parents of our lads are way too nice. Though to be fair,
Gio's mum might be useful in a scrap. For a moment, my
stomach hollows and my throat dries. It's like being in a
pub when you hear that first tinkle of broken glass. Your
body somehow knows there is going to be trouble.

Luckily, as the ref turns and marches back on to the
pitch, instead of hitting him, their manager simply throws
his arms out and, with mock exasperation, shouts:

'Ref, you're having a laugh.'

But he isn't.

From there, things take a turn from bad to embarrassing. As the opposition's temper boils, the referee takes
their every complaint as proof of guilt, their every moan
as a challenge to his integrity. He starts to give some decisions in our favour which you don't need Andy Gray and
his mega slo-mo replays to know should not have gone
our way. With each dodgy ruling, over on the far touchline, the opposition parents' blood pressure bubbles off
the scale. Every single one of them is shouting abuse.
Anyone strolling on to the park now would shake their
head and think, Ah, right, so this is boys' football, mad
parents shouting, of course. Even the bloke in the Barbour
has lost all connection with reason.

Following their parents and coach's example, the opposition players have lost it too. Lost sight of their purpose,
lost sight of the game. And what worries me is they are
taking out their frustrations on my players' shins. Lee has

just hobbled off in tears, a lump the size and colour of a Victoria plum blooming just below his shinpad.

In amongst it all, in the middle of this madness, the referee appears to be having the time of his life. The whistle sounds continually. Cards are fluttering in the breeze. The manager is spoken to three times. Things reach a bizarre turn when Barney, running back with their centre forward, places an elbow into the lad's ribs to lever him on to the turf. The ref, no more than five yards away from the incident, waves play on, allowing Barney to boot the ball into touch. As he gets up, their player shouts, not unreasonably I think:

'Come on, ref, that was a foul, for God's sake.'

He is booked for bad language.

Thus, as they lose focus in a game we might have lost heavily, slowly we creep into contention. With five minutes to go, we are given a free-kick after Mark is tackled seemingly legitimately. By now, their manager has given up complaining and is just laughing at everything.

'Penalty!' he shouts, his arms outspread in mock exasperation. 'Why don't you give your mates a bleedin' penalty!'

It is just a free-kick which Tim, who has been wonderful throughout the game, smacks home. It is now 1-1 and so fed up are they, I can see them giving up altogether, allowing us to sneak the most unjustified point.

Then, with barely a minute to go, one of their talented forwards finally gets the better of Tim. A desperate Barney upends him just outside the penalty area. The referee, to a sizeable, ironic cheer from the far touchline, gives them a free-kick. Their player hits it high into the goal, Max nowhere near it. My, how they celebrate. There is a pile of their players on top of the goalscorer; on the touchline the manager and the parents leap around, their frustrations finally eased. Oh well, I think, can't say they didn't deserve it.

The referee, however, thinks differently. He stands by the heap of boys and, after the last one has got to his feet, he blows his whistle and says:

'The kick will have to be retaken. I hadn't blown my whistle.'

Which must be a first for this match.

This news does not go down well with our guests. I catch Hamish's eye and he nods in the direction of their manager who has dropped to his knees and is banging his fists on the ground.

Maybe this is final proof that I lack the killer instinct, maybe I am just a wimp, but, as their player lines up the free-kick again, as Tim tries to corral our wall, as Max moves them this way and that, as my son stands there in the middle of it all with his hands clasped over his groin, for the first time I can remember, I'm thinking this of an opponent in a football match: God, I hope they score. God, I hope they score.

The referee blows his whistle. Their player asks him if it's OK to take it and on the nod hammers a shot over the wall towards the net. Max dives across and flaps a hand at it, makes contact and steers it towards the post. It strikes the bottom of the upright and bounces back out into play. For a moment I think they have missed it. But the ball hits a prostrate Max on the back of the head and trickles back over the line.

This time it counts. Thank God, I think. They have won.

Now you might imagine that after all this the referee would sprint off at the end, anxious to seek the refuge of the clubhouse. But no, he strolls, head held high, across the pitch, takes his flags from the two linesmen and makes for the changing rooms, apparently oblivious to the gathering swarm of parents and players swishing around him. All of their supporters take it in turns to inform him he is a disgrace. Actually, according to the Barbour-clad grandfather, he is a 'fucking disgrace'. One of them turns to me and says:

'How much did you pay him, then?'

'Nothing to do with me,' I say. 'He was a league appointment.'

I can see they don't believe me. Then I remember I have actually got to pay him his match fee. Money has got to change hands. I catch up with him outside the clubhouse after I have spoken to our lads, after I have watched Barry do his hanging from the crossbar bit to remove the nets and after I have asked their manager to fill in the match card ('Don't forget to give the ref a mark,' I say, hoping to lighten the mood with a gag; it doesn't work). Before I hand over his fifteen quid, I do a quick look round to check none of them are around. But I've missed a couple of their players and parents coming out of the tea bar. They spot the exchange of cash.

'Told you they were cheats,' one of them shouts over.

'Yeah, disgrace, the lot of them. Should be ashamed,' adds the parent.

The boy then spits in our direction for good measure.

'So,' I say to the ref, not quite sure what the social etiquette is when you have just been spat at. 'Don't suppose we'll be seeing you again after that.'

'Why do you say that?' he says. 'I thoroughly enjoyed myself.'

8

It doesn't get any easier

The first time I ever got involved with kids' football as an adult was when a colleague asked me if I'd help him with his son's birthday party. The lad was football mad and was having a celebratory match in the back garden. I was running the office team at the time, so the colleague fondly imagined I had some sort of competence in the foot-balling area. On the day, I arrived first and he showed me the venue. If not Wembley, it was of a reasonable size, certainly with enough turf to accommodate a dozen or so six-year-olds. He'd managed to purloin some traffic cones from the nearby roadworks, which we set up in pairs as goals, and he had a tin of whitewash which we opened up and used to mark out some wobbly lines (have you ever tried painting lines? I don't want to sound all *Changing Rooms* here, but it's a lot harder than you imagine when you open up that tin, particularly when all you have is a bristle-shedding wallpaper brush). He had also bought some medals and a small silver-coloured trophy, which we placed on a table on the patio. His son, a lad facing the enormity of his sixth birthday with considerable fortitude, was bouncing up and down with anticipation even as the lines were being splodged and the medals arranged.

'I'm Michael Thomas,' he said. 'Who are you?'

'I won't be playing, I don't think, mate.'

'Why?'

'I'm too big.'

'OK. You can be George Graham, then.'

So I said I would be, and, when the lines were done, the kid and I walked back into the house together, to discuss the all-important tactics.

'Daniel can be Alan Smith,' he said. 'And Jake can be that Limpar. Who else plays for Arsenal?'

Soon, the guests began to arrive, spilling through the house and out into the garden, dropped off in the street by parents who waved thankfully from their cars and shot away, off to make the most of a couple of hours gratis babysitting. Then one of the boys arrived with his dad, and the man walked into the house apparently intent on staying. He had in his hand a hold-all.

'Right, where can we get changed?' he said as he walked in.

'Well, I mean, he's only six, do it in here,' my colleague replied, gesticulating round the sitting room.

'No, I think a bit of privacy, don't you?' said the new arrival.

Sensing that the boy was maybe a little shy, my colleague said, sure, yeah, course and led the two of them to the bottom of the stairs and told them to take their pick of bedrooms, or if the boy wanted he could use the bathroom on the left, where there was a lock on the door.

As they disappeared upstairs, I made my way into the garden and was soon failing miserably to apply any sort of order to the proceedings. Within about two minutes, I had rapidly disabused myself of the assumption that sorting out a bunch of six-year-olds would be easy. Already two of the boys were wearing the traffic-cone goalposts as hats, someone had fallen over on the white line and now had paint all the way up his pricey-looking designer shorts and someone else was trying out rugby tackles while telling everyone that his dad had said football was a poof's game. Another lad simply lay down full length on the turf anytime the ball came near him. It was quite an effective tactic at this level; he broke up several opposition attacks that way as the ball seemed attracted to his midriff as if by magnetism. That is when we had a ball. The party was no more than five minutes old when the birthday boy's prized Arsenal ball was hoofed over the fence.

'Don't worry,' said our host, emerging from the house. 'I'll pop round and get it.'

While he was gone, we made do with a flat old leather number I found behind the greenhouse. It was what we used to call a casey when I was a kid, an item that had clearly been hanging around in the garden for ages. The boys could hardly kick the thing it was so heavy, soaked as it was in several seasons of rain, its surface thick with slimy lichen. As the boys ran around the leaden, half-moon-shaped ball, shouting and failing to make it move more than a couple of feet at any one time, an apparition appeared at the back door. It was the newly arrived bloke and his son. And what was so surprising about them was this: in the days before the replica kit explosion, before every kid in the neighbourhood had at least three versions of Chelsea's home shirt, the pair of them were decked out in vintage 1970s Tottenham outfits. Father and son together, right down to the colour-coordinated ties round the top of brilliant white socks.

'Do you think', the father said to me, 'that it will take a stud?'

'I dunno . . . You know, it's just a . . .' I spluttered. 'Nah, I'm sure he'll be fine in trainers, everyone else is.'

'I didn't mean for him,' he said, extracting from a Spurs boot bag he had in his hand a full-sized pair of Nikes. 'I meant for me.'

He then walked on to the middle of the makeshift pitch, just to the point where a small scrum of six-year-olds had formed round the boy who liked to lie prostrate on the turf. He bent to his knees, pushed his thumb into the ground in a screwing motion and announced:

'Better safe than sorry.'

A couple of minutes later, after he had tied the laces on his boots, slipped his shin pads into his socks and windmilled his arms around by way of a warm-up, he marched on to the pitch. Quickly – and not unreasonably – realising that I was having no effect on the organisational side of things, he took charge.

'Right,' he said. 'I'll have Dominic, Daniel, you, you and you on my side. Everyone else is on the oppostion. You're Arsenal, we're Tottenham, it's the third round of the FA Cup and this, ladies and gentlemen, is White Hart Lane.'

'OK and what shall I—' I said.

'You? Oh, just stand in front of the greenhouse, you know, in case the windows . . .'

And so the game kicked off, with Spurs immediately imposing themselves on the fray, largely because their midfield maestro was about three times the size of any of the opposition. I watched from the greenhouse door as the big lad in the middle showed them no quarter, scattering small boys in his wash as he stamped around the garden, reckless and ruthless.

'Free-kick,' he yelled, as his son fell over in one of the few melees that did not involve him. 'I'll take it and you'll need a wall.'

A couple of the boys in the Arsenal team looked at me for advice, so I stepped in to arrange them into a defensive line, with the birthday boy at its heart. And with the lad who liked to lie down lying down behind them. It appeared immediately to be an unequal struggle, a bunch of six-year-olds − one of them lying down − facing a man in his thirties who looked like the sort whose idea of fun was firing a couple of underlings before his morning coffee had cooled.

'Ten yards, I think,' he said, waving his hand at the wall.

'Yeah but . . .' I said. 'The whole pitch isn't much more than that.'

'Whatever, they've got to be further back than that.'

So I shuffled and rolled them a foot or so towards their own goal, then stood off the pitch and watched him place the ball carefully on the turf. He took five measured steps backwards, stopped, looked at the small boy standing between the two cones, looked back at the ball, looked at the boy again, then ran up and smacked it as hard as he could in the direction of his opponents' goal. Though he struck it well enough, it didn't travel far. In fact it spun no more than three or four yards before wrapping itself, like the beast unleashed from the bowels of the mother ship in the *Alien* movies, around the face of the birthday boy standing in the wall. For a split second nothing moved, then, with his head remaining perfectly still, the lad's feet came up off the ground until they were almost parallel with his chin. He fell flat on to the turf, his hands, rather late in the day, moving up from his groin to protect his face. No one budged, so I stepped forward, knelt down over the poleaxed kid and assessed the damage. At least the awful wail coming from out of his mouth indicated he was conscious.

'Let me have a look,' I said, trying to prise apart his fingers. 'Come on, let me see.'

Finally he opened his fingers up enough for me to spot that his face was an unholy mess, smeared in a slimy cock-tail of damp leather, lichen, blood, snot and tears. His nose was obviously broken.

'What the hell . . .' I heard our host shout as he came running back into the garden with the retrieved Arsenal ball under his arm, to be confronted by what appeared to be the opening scene from *Casualty*.

'Oh God, I'm sorry, I'm so sorry,' said the big man as he leaned over me to peer at the mangled face. 'But I did warn them they weren't the full ten yards.'

Those boys will now be in their mid-twenties. You'd recognise my colleague's son if you ever met him. He's the one with the nose up by his right eyebrow. For all I know, he and a couple of his mates might even now be pacing the touchline of their local park, watching their own kids hack around on a Sunday morning. The bloke who fancied himself as Glen Hoddle is these days running some worldwide conglomerate and my former colleague is a successful media face. Everyone has moved on. Except me. Me, I'm still trying to organise a bunch of boys into playing a game of football.

And I'm not getting any better at it.

In fact, as things are going at the moment I think I'm getting worse. Each and every week we are being beaten. We have so far played seven games and lost six of them. The only win we recorded was discounted after the opposition folded. We are second bottom of the table, kept from the very basement by a team that has by some miracle of incompetence conceded even more goals than us. And we don't play them until next month.

The thing is, I just don't know what to do. Shane Warne reckons that the definition of a good team coach is that the big vehicle that takes players to and from the stadium is well stocked with cigarettes, cheese sandwiches and DVDs. And he might be right. Far from adding value to the team, I seem to be wholly irrelevant. Maybe even counterproductive. These are not physical incompetents I have in my side. Several of them are very athletic: Ryan can run like a whippet, Lee has the balance of a gazelle, Adam can do so many keepy-uppies even he loses count. As for Tim, well. Every week he is just magnificent: quick, strong, astonishingly committed in all he does. When he won the player of the season last year I said at the presentation evening that he wasn't a boy, he was a man. And he is, our Duncan Edwards. Yet, though I have all these footballers, these good players, these stalwarts of their school teams at my disposal, I seem incapable of turning them into any kind of potent force.

It is not through want of trying. At training we spend hours working on passing and moving. That's what all the experts I have asked tell me is the best way to do it: make sure everyone gets plenty of time on the ball, play in small groups, keep things fast-paced, keep up their attention. And they look great on a Thursday night, in their small-sided games of two-touch and three-touch and silent football, full of skill and endeavour, leaving me, whenever I join in, panting in their shadows. Yet when it comes to matches, they seem to panic and revert to playing like they did when they were eight, hoofing the ball anywhere in the vague hope that something might develop. Actually, I'm not sure they even think that. They give every appearance of merely not wanting to be in possession of the ball.

In my team talks I try to keep things simple, restrict the ideas to just one or two points – pass to a man in the same colour shirt, close the opposition down when they have possession and when you get a chance, bury it. The lads seem to listen, then go out and pass to someone wearing a different-coloured shirt, stand back when the opposition has control and, when they are one on one with the keeper, pad the ball politely into his midriff.

Track back and mark, I say beforehand, then spend half the match yelling at Luke or Faisal to track back and mark. It is as if they are waiting for me to shout before they set off. One week I think maybe their response is becoming mechanical, Pavlovian; they are subconsciously waiting for the shout. So the next week I try not shouting. It makes no difference whatsoever: still nobody tracks back.

In fact, so badly are we doing, I'm beginning to think like Don Revie. The former Leeds and England manager was absolutely convinced fate was the most potent force in football. So he wore the same suit every week, he ate the same pre-match meal, he insisted the team bus took the same route to the ground; he would do nothing to challenge the celestial powers he reckoned governed the game. When things went wrong, he assumed he had offended the fates and spent hours racking his brain to work out what he had done to provoke their disapproval.

Right now, I must have run over a cattery of black moggies, or butchered the local population of magpies, or walked under a street-full of ladders. Because our luck is woeful. We attack and hit the post and the ball bounces back into the keeper's arms; they attack and hit the post and it bounces off the back of our keeper's head into the goal. The ball bobbles around in their penalty area from a corner and it just won't land at any of our players' feet. Our lads swish and slash and just can't connect. But when the ball bobbles around in our area, it falls perfectly on the laces of their centre forward's right boot, enabling him to blast it into the net. We make a mistake and it is punished. They just don't make mistakes.

This is the time a coach can – should – must – make a difference. Except I stand on the touchline watching the lads falter every week and I don't know what to do. I've tried encouraging, I've tried bollocking; I know for certain sarcasm doesn't work, so I just keep encouraging to no visible reward. Perhaps I should be more active tactically, switching them from 4-4-2 to 4-3-3 to counteract the threat of the opposition's wing-backs. But even when I do spot something, I don't react quickly enough. My tactical response generally comes a day or so after the final whistle, when I'm on the escalator on my way to the office or just buying a latte at the coffee store round the corner and it comes to me in a flash: of course, I needed to put Barney in central midfield just to stop their big lad running the game. Stop his supply and we'd have been all right. Next time I'll try and think of that seventy-two hours earlier.

Actually, the truth is, I'm useless at watching the opposition. I spend my whole time looking at how we are playing, my eyes scanning from Paul to Barney to Tim to Lee back to Barney. I don't seem to be able to take in the opposing players, to work out who is a threat. Barry sometimes says things to me like: That blond-haired lad's getting too much space. And I think, Which blond-haired lad? I hadn't even noticed a blond-haired lad.

In fact, sometimes it has got so bad, I don't even recognise my own players.

'Luke, for God's sake, don't waste possession like that,' I yelled the other day as a small figure appeared suddenly to go transparent and let a nicely hit pass from Adam go right through him.

'It wasn't me,' came an indignant voice a good thirty yards from the action. 'I'm over here.'

After the game, I sought him out.

'Sorry, Luke,' I said. 'I must be going blind.'

Luke, a lad of such sunny disposition he could no more hold a grudge than he could keep possession, generously accepted my apology.

'That's OK. If it had've been me, I'd've probably missed it an' all,' he said.

Last week, I reached my coaching nadir. We were playing in a village outside town. As it happens, village is something of a misnomer. This was not honey-coloured stone cottages clustered round a green, with smoke snaking out of the chimney pots and old boys dressed in plus fours leaning on gateposts chewing straw. This was slum clearance refugees plonked in the middle of nowhere in prefabricated pebble-dashed semis, with smoke snaking out of tin foil round the back of the bus shelter, and gangs of youths in hoodies leaning on vandalised phone boxes chewing gum. Every ten minutes or so, jets from the nearby RAF station rumbled over on their way to bully Iraq or Afghanistan or Kosovo, rattling the ribcage as they passed seemingly within touching distance, scattering livestock in their downdraught and rendering any attempt at conversation pointless. It is the kind of place no one ever goes to except to play football.

Not that we are playing much today. Midway through the game, even I could see this problem unfolding: their winger was advancing with the ball and their midfielders were flooding through the middle of the pitch, nicely in position for a cross or a cut-back. They were queuing up, all totally unmarked on the edge of the area, because our midfielders were standing in the centre circle watching them run. Not one of our lads was tracking back. Not one. I tried to shout out a warning but instead found myself yelling:

'For fu . . . look . . . gah . . . Barney!'

Barney shot me a pained look as he realised it was him against four, a mini-Alamo unfolding under the RAF's flight path.

Fortunately their player took the wrong option, the cross went behind for a goal kick and I turned to Barry and said:

'I've lost the ability to speak.'

To which he said: 'Bloody hell. You?'

I could see his point. About the only thing I've ever been able to do properly in football is shout. When I was a player, I was less renowned for my performance than for my volume. It reached a point where I was taken aside by Robert, my sometime partner at centre back. He was elegant, languorous, skilful on the ball and the two of us formed an unlikely double act: Mr Quiet and Mr Shouty. After one particularly fraught game, in which I had spent so much time trying to get my team-mates to put in a bit more effort that I had bawled myself hoarse, he sought me out over the post-match pint. He was, he said, speaking on behalf of the rest of the lads.

'I know you put in a lot of effort for the team, but we were wondering if it were absolutely necessary to, erm, you know, as it were, shout so much?' he said, sounding like Sergeant Wilson advising Captain Mainwaring.

'I mean,' he continued, 'do you think it's actually getting us anywhere?'

Now I can't even shout.

Can't shout.

Can't coach.

Can't win.

'It's not just about winning,' my wife tells me when she comes into the kitchen one evening and sees me staring into space. Sitting there, staring at nothing.

And she's right. It's not just about winning. Just a draw would do.

9

It's a knockout

I raise the subject with Barney on the way home from training.

'Good session, that.'

'Yeah.'

'Everyone looked up for it.'

'Yeah.'

'So how come we couldn't play like that on Sunday?'

'Dunno.'

'We can't keep losing like we are.'

'We won't.'

'If we keep losing, we'll lose all our good players. Tim'll definitely go.'

I've already seen at least one rival manager, after a game, approach Tim and tell him how well he's played and said if he ever wants to join a decent club, to give him a call. In the Premier League they'd launch an inquiry into tapping up. But I see it and think, It's only a matter of time. Barney thinks differently. He gives me a look. That you-know-nothing look teenaged boys reserve for their fathers.

'Dad, do you know Tim?' he says.

'You don't think?'

'No. No way. He is this team.'

There's a pause.

'Anyhow,' he says, 'we'll be all right when Kal gets back fit again. We'll be fine.'

'Do you reckon?'

'Yeah, course,' he says.

There is silence in the car for a moment or two.

'Mind you,' he adds. 'We could use a goalie.'

Ah yes, the goalkeeper problem.

There is always the goalkeeper problem in kids' football. It sits there, squatting over every match you play, the great unspoken, the elephant in the goalmouth. Actually, it would be great if there really were an elephant in the goalmouth. At least then it might get in the way of the odd shot. Unlike some of the keepers we've had.

No one wants to be a keeper, that's the root of it. At age seven, every kid wants the glory of goal-scoring. They want to be the guy slamming the ball into the net, then peeling off to conduct a complicated mimed celebration featuring a bow and a quiver full of arrows. Not the guy picking the ball out of the net while all the parents yell at him that it's his fault. It is bad enough persuading a lad that his future might lie at left back. At least every so often the left back will venture over the halfway line. But a goalie? The only way they'll go in is if they are mad or you tell them to. And like *Catch-22*, if they say yes when you tell them to, that merely proves they are mad.

So what happens is this: the fat kid gets put in goal. Or the kid whose parents realise he won't get in the team otherwise. Or the kid who thinks he's great everywhere but more often than not, isn't. Brian Clough based his whole tactical approach to the game on this one certainty: it all starts with the goalie. That's why he spent half his career trying to sign Peter Shilton. And couldn't stop smiling when he did.

When we started out, our first custodian – as Big Ron calls them – was Timothy, whose dad claimed he had once been a keeper himself. Slight and shy, we called him Tiny Tim to differentiate him from Big Tim, who even back then was our colossus. Tiny Tim was never remotely going to be a keeper. Ever. Not if we played until the sun froze over or Roman Abramovich ran out of loose change would he be a keeper. But no one else wanted to go in, so Tiny Tim got the job.

Of his several drawbacks perhaps the most significant was that Tiny Tim was scared of the ball. While even as an eight-year-old, Paul enjoyed the physicality of the game, enjoyed flinging himself into the fray, if truth be told secretly enjoyed inflicting pain on an opponent, you could see by his every step that Tiny Tim really wished he was anywhere other than on a football field, in goal, with a member of the opposing team dribbling towards him. Peter Schmeichel used to keep goal by flinging himself at the ball, happy to stop it with whatever part of his body he could. Face, hands, backside: he didn't care. When someone bore down on Tiny Tim's goal, the boy would do whatever was necessary to get his body out of the way. On a couple of occasions I saw him swivelling his hips like a matador just to ensure there was absolutely no contact whatsoever between him and that hard, hurty thing heading in his direction. Boy, did he move well.

He lasted about three months in the under-nines before his dad phoned me to say he was taking up ballet, so couldn't come along any more. And I thought, Well, he's got the hip movement for it. I don't think of all of us concerned there was anyone more relieved at that news than Tiny Tim.

Our next keeper was Rufus. He turned up at the beginning of the next season with his friend, Patrice. Patrice, whose French dad had married a local girl he first met during a school exchange, had a delightful touch and a left foot which could bring pattern and order to the most shambolic of nine-year-olds' kickarounds. When Patrice had the ball, almost invariably he did something good with it. From the moment I saw him trap a ball, I wanted Patrice to play for us. But, after he had come along to a couple of training sessions to see how he enjoyed it, his dad said Patrice would only sign if Rufus signed up too. Patrice and Rufus were a transfer double act. Except you could tell that from the first kickaround theirs was a partnership of unequals, more Little and Large than Ardiles and Villa. But I thought, Why not? We had a couple of places, anything was worth getting Patrice in the squad and also Rufus said he'd go in goal.

Rufus was what my mum would call a really well brought-up young man. He was polite, friendly, kind; when he smiled, the whole world brightened up. He was one of nature's good sorts. A lovely guy. And that was his problem. He was a big lad, tall, wide, big hands, a goalie's build. But he was loath to use his scale. In fact, it seemed to embarrass him. Rather than dominate, you could see him trying to shrink down to everyone else's size. He was, basically, too nice. Way too nice. I've met some proper goalkeepers in my time and none of them could be described as too nice.

Mainly Rufus was this: he was sorry. I have never heard anyone apologise on a football field as much as Rufus did.

'Sorry,' he'd say when he'd flapped at a cross and missed it.

'Sorry,' he'd say when he'd got nowhere near a piledriver.

I even once heard him say sorry to the opposition forward who he had upended diving for the ball.

'Sorry. You OK? Didn't mean to do that. Sorry,' he said. And I thought, Hang on, why didn't you mean to do it?

I used to try to rev him up before matches: 'C'mon, Rufy, really impose yourself, shout your name out when you go to catch it, make yourself big, c'mon, get angry, be Mr Nasty.'

And he'd go, 'Grrr', then break into his big, gentle smile.

Then he'd get out on the pitch and the first thing he'd do is say:

'Sorry. Should have been my ball. Sorry.'

Jeff used to say to me back then, after one of our regular Rufus apologies, 'You've got to get rid of him, he's useless, we'll never win anything with him.'

And I'd say: 'Oh come on, he's a great kid.'

But secretly I knew he had a point.

Rufus did too. Kind, diffident, polite he might have been but one thing he wasn't was stupid. He could hear the sighs from the touchline when he mishit a clearance; he could read the look Tim gave him when he didn't claim a cross; he knew who Kal was referring to when he shouted, 'C'mon on lads, we can do better than this', after the opposition had scored the softest of goals. And I don't think I did much for his self-esteem when I shouted out, 'Come on, Rufus, make a bloody effort', when he stood stock-still in the middle of the goal and watched the ball head for the corner of his net.

Perhaps the biggest surprise was that he lasted nearly three seasons in goal before his mum approached me after training once and asked if it might be possible for Rufy perhaps to have a game or two on the pitch.

'Only if that's OK with you,' she said. 'Sorry to be a nuisance.'

I was happy to give him a go. But out on the field his niceness got in the way of every tackle. After a few months of turning up less and less often to training, of usually having an excuse why he couldn't make it on Sunday, his mum rang me again to deliver the hardly unexpected news that he was dropping out. He was going to take up rowing, she said. He fancied a sport that he could do sitting down, she said. 'Sorry,' she said.

I was really sorry, too, to see him leave. Partly I was sorry because he was a person of such benevolence, he cheered you up just being in the same county as him. But mainly it was because he took Patrice with him to the rowing club.

So we were keeper-less, Fraser filling in occasionally, Barney too standing in. Then one day last summer, Tim (who no longer had need of the 'Big' soubriquet since his namesake took up pirouettes on a Sunday morning) turned up at training saying he'd found us a goalie. Max was new to the area, and had just enrolled in Tim's school. He was another nice kid, with an open, kind face. I knew he'd fit in with the boys, and if Tim was championing him, I thought he must be good. He played in a summer six-a-side tournament when I was away one weekend and Barry phoned me afterwards to say he was just the man. We had got to the final and he'd saved a couple of penalties on the way there.

'I tell you what, he's a shot-stopper,' said Bazz.

Plus, he could be very funny, full of jokes, usually at his own expense. I thought he'd do for me.

But the thing was, by the time the season started, he had only played in six-a-side tournaments, or at training, both of which used small goals. When we reverted back to big pitches, eleven-a-side and full-sized nets, he suddenly looked very small and frail, a look made worse by the fact he was wearing Rufus's old goalkeeping shirt, which hung from him like Demis Roussos's kaftan.

Despite his lack of substance, he began reasonably well. If not very confident with a high ball, he made a few good saves on the ground. But over the last few weeks, I've been watching his confidence ebb away. He hasn't been coming to training and missed a couple of our recent games. Rory's dad had a word with me the last time we played saying he was worried by the boy's body language.

'He looks scared,' he said. 'I don't think he's enjoying himself.'

Today is not a day for a goalkeeper with shot nerves. It is the second round of the county cup. We had a bye through the first, though given our current condition, it was a surprise we didn't lose that. We are drawn against an established A League team, a side who seem to win most of the six-a-side tournaments we play in every summer. They have a centre forward who is renowned locally for his size and ability. According to Barry, our local pro club have been trying to sign him for years, but he's always resisted their approaches. He's holding out for a big-time team, Barry reckons. He is just the sort of player who could destroy us in our present state.

But then, two things happen during the warm-ups that make me think that our luck might be changing. First I see Kal trotting across the field in kit, ready to play. Then, as I walk past them, warming up in their neat matching tracksuits, I can't see their big guy. It's not that he is hard to miss. I look again. He definitely isn't there.

'Got a full squad?' I say to their manager, the note of hope evident in my voice.

'Nah, missing our centre forward,' their man says.

'That's a blow,' I say, trying not to sound too ecstatic.

'Doesn't worry us,' he says. 'You should see the size of the lad who's replacing him.'

The big lad wasn't in their line-up the last time we played them either. It, too, was a cup match a couple of seasons back, when we were still in the B League and, in perhaps our greatest performance ever as a team, with Tim and Kal and Barney and Paul tackling everything that moved, we managed to beat them. It is clearly a defeat that is still preying on their manager's mind.

'I just overheard their bloke talking to them when I walked past,' Barry tells me as we all gather. 'He told them to remember what happened last time, how we'd outfought them in the midfield and how it mustn't happen again. He said we embarrassed them.'

Which gives me an idea. I gather the boys together, tell them their positions, tell them who is starting substitute, then, instead of saying the usual stuff they don't listen to anyway, I try a bit of psychology:

'They're scared of you. They remember last time you played them and they're terrified it's going to happen again. Bazz just heard their manager say that our midfield is the hardest they've had to play in the past three years.'

The boys look suspicious. Tim looks at Gio as if someone has just told him that the bloke down the chip shop has just had the results of his DNA test back and it turns out he really is Elvis.

'Didn't he, Bazz?' I say.

'Definitely,' says Barry. 'They're scared of you, boys.'

So this is what it is like not to lose.

This is what it is like to compete, to create, to have a bit of luck. To have your chief midfielder fit. This is what it is like to play against the best in the county and match them.

Even without an absent Paul and Rory, we harass them and chase them and scare them. We even start to play a bit, passing the ball, moving into space, creating chances. My half-time team talk doesn't consist of shouts or gee-ups or leaping up and down on the spot. The only noise coming out of my mouth sounds suspiciously like purring.

On the touchline, the volume has returned. Hamish has refound his 'grrrrrrr'. Mike, the under-twelves manager, has stopped to watch after his game has finished and is bawling out non-stop praise. Alan, Mark's stepdad and a man who just a month ago told me he is that rare sort of bloke for whom football does absolutely nothing at all, is doing a very good impression of a lifelong obsessive. Even my wife is there, occasionally telling our friend who is staying the weekend to 'look at my husband, what does he think he looks like?'

One of their parents has a video camera and most of the action he is filming is in his own team's half as we press and harry. With ten minutes to go, we are 2-0 up and I'm beginning to think this is easy.

But it isn't. Max, who has not had much to do all morning, scuffs at a back pass from Tim. The ball spins to their stand-in forward who, perhaps surprised at the gift, doesn't properly connect with a shot goalwards. Max, though, misjudges his dive and the ball whimpers into the net.

Encouraged by a roar from their supporters, they push on. With just a minute left and panic beginning to afflict our defence, someone shoots from distance. Like wet soap, it squirms through Max's hands.

It's 2-2.

I barely have time to register the look on Tim's face before the whistle goes. As the boys gather, I know what I'm going to say. I have just read a biography of Sir Alf Ramsey which recalled what he said at the same stage in the 1966 World Cup final. It is the most renowned bit of on-pitch oratory in the English game, and I pinch it, wholesale:

'You've won it once. So just go out there and win it again.'

That is the thing about fourteen-year-olds: they are cliché virgins. Though it might be the most well-worn bit of advice in the game, none of them has heard it before. It works. Tim leads the response:

'That's it, lads, we have won it already. We can do it again, c'mon,' he says, clapping his hands together.

As they are heading back out on to the pitch, I catch Max by the elbow.

'Unlucky, mate, one of those things,' I say.

'Told you I wasn't a keeper,' he says.

'No, you didn't. I thought you were.'

'No, I'm left midfield.'

This is news I don't want to hear right now.

'Hey, just keep concentrating . . .'

Those who say extra time goes in a flash have obviously never managed a team through it. Time drags, time congeals, time turns into a stodgy, thickening gloop. It seems to go on for hours as two exhausted teams thrash and hack. Thank goodness we are allowed rolling substitutions; it means Barry can patch up Ryan and Lee when they limp off and send them back into the fray. With about five minutes to go, he is pressed into urgent action. A swift bit of passing on the edge of our area releases their big stand-in. Barney and Tim are stranded, he strides into the box, rounds Max easily and has his leg triggered ready to smack home the winner when from nowhere Kal slides in and dispossesses him. A piece of defending that has even their supporters applauding. But there are consequences. In the execution of the tackle, Kal's ankle has gone yet again. He is carried to the touchline where his father and Barry look at his foot and shake their heads in unison. With the end approaching, the consequence of his absence suddenly dawns on me. There are no replays in this cup; ties are decided by penalty shoot-out. Kal is our penalty taker. He simply never misses. And he is not on the pitch.

'Barry,' I shout. 'Get him back on, we need him for the penalties.'

'He can't walk.'

'I don't care, get him back on for the penalties.'

'Honest, he can't walk.'

'Doesn't need to walk to take a penalty, get him back on.'

'Excuse me a moment.' It's Mike, the under-twelves manager.

'What?'

'Speaking as the club's child protection officer, I don't think you should be jeopardising a boy's health and safety like that.'

'Are you joking?'

'No.'

'Well, I'm the chairman, get him back on.'

But it's too late. The whistle has gone. Penalties it is. And without Kal. Or Adam, our other sure-fire scorer, who is also off the pitch, holding a swelling knee.

We gather in the centre circle, where Lee is first to speak.

'I'm not taking one,' he says.

'Sure?' I say.

'Yeah, I'm not taking one.'

'OK, who actually wants to take one?'

Only Luke volunteers.

'Well done, Lukey,' I say. 'Right, so we'll go Luke, Jamie, Mark, Tim. And Franz can take the last one. You're German, so you won't miss.'

And so it begins. Its simplicity is up there with the 100m dash or the heavyweight championship bout; no sub-plots, no diversions, no offside to confuse the issue, just one man against another, scoring to win the game. Or in the case of England over the years, missing to lose it.

Everyone can understand the penalty shoot-out, its logic is utterly insistent. When one is on the television, the viewing figures go through the roof as those who have taken themselves off to potter in the garden or attend to their sock draw during the inconclusive one hundred and twenty minutes of sweat and nonsense that have preceded it, return to watch its plot unfold. Now there is one in our local park. It is every bit as emotionally draining. My wife finds it almost unbearable.

'Oh God,' she says as she stands by my shoulder. 'I hope no one misses.'

'Well, someone has to, otherwise it'll go on all night.'

'No, I can't bear it. It's too much for boys this age.'

They go first. It's their smallest player.

'He'll miss,' says Barry.

He scores. Then Luke, his mind for once focused on something other than his next bit of tomfoolery, scores. They score again. Then Jamie scores, his dad completely unable to watch, crouching on his haunches, hands covering his face. And so it goes on, everyone scoring, until it is their last man's turn. He steps up. Both sets of players are on the halfway line, their arms round each other in the manner they have seen on the telly, watching him walk forward. He picks up the ball and re-spots it. He steps back.

'He'll miss,' says Barry.

And he does. His shot high and wide. As the ball settles in the bush behind the goal, he bursts into tears.

'Oh God, it's cruel,' says my wife. She turns to Mike:

'I thought you were the child protection officer. Can't you stop this?'

It is Franz next. If he scores, we win. He's German. He won't miss. There is a slight step forward of our line as he walks to the spot, the boys are on their toes, ready to run and celebrate. He turns. He runs forward. He kicks the ball towards the corner of the goal. And their keeper stretching, diving, desperate, knocks the ball on to the post and out. The kid who was blubbing a moment before is the first to rush forward and congratulate the keeper.

'Did you get that?' their manager shouts at the parent with the video camera.

'Think so,' he says. 'Hope so.'

And I'm thinking, Where did they find a goalkeeper like that?

'What now?' says my wife.

'Sudden death,' I say.

'Oh God,' she says. 'I think I'll be the first to die if this goes on.'

They take the first penalty and score. Their parents yelp with relief. First up for us is Barn.

'Jesus,' I whisper.

'Give the lad a break,' says Mike. 'He'll score.'

I can't watch. My stomach has the feel of a scrunched-up dishcloth. I can't swallow. The last time Barney took a penalty in a shoot-out he was the only one to miss and couldn't stop sobbing. He strides up confidently. Picks up the ball. Squeezes it. Places it on the spot. Takes a short run up and pops it neatly in the top corner of the goal. I do no more than nod, but inside my guts are auditioning for the next series of *Strictly Come Dancing*. My wife kisses me, Mike shakes me by the hand. But I've done nothing.

And then it happens. Max has got nowhere near a single penalty so far. He has been a spectator, often from the wrong side of the goal after diving in the opposite direction to the ball. Now he is facing their keeper who runs up and shoots hard directly where Max is standing. It is heading for his nose. Instinctively, protectively, he moves his hands up to his face. The ball hits his wrists and is diverted over the crossbar. He has saved it. On our touchline the parents cheer themselves hoarse. Hamish goes, 'Grrrrr'.

Now all we have to do is score the next penalty. But first we have to find someone to take it. There is no movement from the group on the halfway line. Then they form a huddle. Eventually, clearly reluctantly, Lee steps forward. He is our most gifted player but he is also the smallest, our most injury-prone, our least self-confident. He looks tiny as he makes his way to the area, his toes pointing inwards, his shoulders down. Their keeper, desperate to make amends for his miss, is bouncing on the goal line, his arms flapping by his side.

'I can't see him scoring, he looks terrified,' I say to my wife.

Not for the first, or indeed the last, time in my managerial career, I am wrong.

Emphatically, totally and utterly wrong. Lee blasts the ball into the net. There follows all that you might expect. Tears and dismay share the pitch with laughter and shouting. There are human pyramids of delight next to the slumped and dispirited. I find their manager and shake his hand.

'Terrible way for fourteen-year-olds to lose,' I say.

'Hey, one of those things,' he says. 'But I tell you what, we missed our forward.'

Then, as our team mob Lee, as Luke's dad runs round in small circles with his arms held out wide like an aeroplane, as Barry stands there smiling saying to anyone who'll listen, 'I do not know why he won't take them. He never misses when we play in the park', I seek out Max.

'Max,' I say. 'Brilliant, son. You're a keeper now, hey.'

'Yeah,' he says.

But I can't help noticing, as I give him a congratulatory pat on the shoulder, that he is shaking. Shaking like Shakin' Stevens's trousers.

10

Winning

Things have turned on the pitch. Thanks largely to a sudden benevolent streak in the fixture list, we have just enjoyed a winning run, beating a village team in the next round of the cup, and taking our first six points in the league, picked up in home and away victories against the bottom team. Three wins on the bounce, on the march, unheard-of joy. Happy days. Happy, happy days. Nothing more to be said.

Except that no one else in the whole wide world understands and merely assumes that the extra spring in my step means I've had a pay rise. Which is roughly what I have been telling anyone who asks. It's a lot simpler than explaining the real cause.

Imagine it.

'Yeah, I'm smiling because we've just won three on the bounce.'

'Who, United? But hang on, I thought they just lost at West Ham.'

'No, not United. Northmeadow Youth Under-Fourteens.'

'Ah,' they would say. 'And they are?'

'The boys' team I manage.'

And they would look at me in a new and not altogether favourable way.

'Right, OK, got you,' they'd say. 'Must dash.'

11

Keeping things buoyant

When, during an interview, I asked Ron Atkinson his advice about running a boys' football team, he told me to make sure everyone had fun at training.

'For me a player laughing and joking is a happy player. And a happy player is a good player,' he said. 'So I liked training to have a little razz, liked to keep things buoyant.'

After three wins the mood at training tonight is so buoyant you could float Big Ron's gin palace on it. The boys can't stop laughing.

And Ron was right. Even as they laugh, they seem to be running a bit harder, their passing is a bit crisper, they are tackling a bit more ferociously. At one point I play an old Cloughie trick. I tell them that some time, any time, on a prearranged signal of three blasts on the whistle, they must all run away and hide. The whistle could come at any moment, during any drill, I say. But the last one out of my sight does twenty press-ups. I leave it for an age and then blow the whistle in the middle of the five-a-side game at the end of the session. For a moment they are static, wondering what's going on. Adam is the first to

remember the disappearing act and charges off. The rest
fly off after him, ducking into the clubhouse, behind a
tree, through the gap in the hedge. There is pushing and
jostling, aimless hurtling. They look, as they dash in a
dozen different directions at once, like a Keystone Kops
instructional video. To nobody's surprise, it is Luke who
loses. His idea of hiding is to stand behind a goalpost,
where all but a pole-shaped line running down the middle
of his body is clearly visible. And just in case I've missed
him, he flaps his arms up and down as if guiding a plane
along a runway.

'Luke, I can see you.'

'Aw,' he says. As if it wasn't his plan to be the centre
of attention all along.

I think, as they gather round watching Luke flounder
through his press-ups, with Gio jumping on his shoulders at one point and everyone cackling, that Jeff – my
old coaching partner – would have hated this. I don't
often think about him. But at this moment I do, and
that's what I think about him: he would have hated
this.

Jeff believed training should be conducted in an atmosphere of dedication, learning, respect, monastic restraint.
And when it didn't work out like that – which was pretty
much always – he would be sent into a tailspin. I'd get
home after he'd taken a drill or two, or maybe after we'd
split the group into defence and attack and he'd been in
control of the defenders, and I'd wait for him to call. No
more than half an hour after I'd returned, the phone
would ring.

'Can I have a word?' he'd say. 'Training was pathetic
tonight. They don't take it seriously. They don't show
respect. I won't have messing about in my sessions. Won't

stand for it. You've got to do something. You're the manager, you've got to cut it out if we're going to get anywhere with this lot.'

So the next week I'd split the group according to those who would wind Jeff up and those who wouldn't. I'd give him the quiet and sensible ones and take the jokers and show-offs myself. It didn't stop the calls.

'Why did I get all the deadbeats tonight?' he'd say.

'Well, I thought . . .'

'They've no get up and go. They'll never make footballers, not one of them.'

On one occasion I'd had to work late, so I asked him if he could step in and take charge of the whole session. He said he would, no problem. I eventually turned up towards the end of the evening to pick up Barney, only to find Rory and Luke on their own over in the corner of the AstroTurf pitch, sitting on the base of a floodlighting pylon. They had that look on their faces that small boys effortlessly master: the one of wounded innocence.

'What are you two doing?' I said as I walked over to them while Jeff was trying to explain to the others how to spring the offside trap.

'He sent us here,' Rory said, apparently unable to speak Jeff's name.

'Why?'

'Dunno.'

'Well, there must be a reason. What had you done?'

'Nothing.'

'Well, if you did nothing, why did he send you here?'

'Ask him.'

So I did.

'What did those two do?' I said as I walked over to

find Jeff with his head in his hands in despair at the boys' inability to grasp the idea of running out together, arms aloft, on his call.

'Them? The usual. Messing around. Mucking it up for those who want to take it seriously.'

'Yeah, but what did they do?'

'Playing the fool. Not putting any effort in. No discipline. I've spent ages looking up training drills on the internet and they can't be bothered. I mean, do they want to learn?'

'Jeff, they're eleven.'

'Twelve.'

'Well, some are still eleven. But that's not what I—'

'Doesn't matter. Some here want to learn, others don't. We should get rid of those that don't.'

'Yeah, well, I know but it's—'

'Get rid of half this lot and get some in who want to learn.'

Get rid: I'd heard that solution before. Get rid of the middle-class softies. Get rid of Lee, he's just out for himself. Get rid of Kal as skipper and give the armband to someone who'll talk. He's too quiet: get rid. He's too noisy: get rid. He's too selfish: get rid.

'OK, I'll have a word,' I said. And as I walked over to the two boys, sulking and muttering to each other, I thought, What am I doing? Is this really how I want to spend my Wednesday evenings, trying to be the peacemaker in someone else's spat?

'Right, fellas,' I said. 'Do me a favour, eh. Just take it seriously, yeah?'

'Well, tell him to stop picking on us,' said Rory.

'Come on, mate, I'm sure he's not—'

'He is. It's always us. Never his son. Oh no.'

'Hey, no, no, no it's not . . . I don't think . . . That's not . . .'

But there was no real arguing with him. That was precisely what it was all about. That was at the core of it all. It was all about father and son. It is always about father and son.

We know that this is the way boys' football operates: it is the dad of one of the squad who becomes the manager or helps with the coaching. And with that comes inevitable tensions, with that comes politics, with that comes problems for the boy and the father. If the manager's son is the best player in the team, then that can be problematic: it makes the other boys feel that the whole thing is just the dad and his lad show. But what is far worse is if the team think that the boy doesn't pull his weight, if they reckon he isn't good enough and the coach – through natural parental affection – plays him anyway. Or never substitutes him. Or puts him as centre forward when he couldn't hit the target if he had a laser guidance system fitted into his boots. Or won't allow him to take up his ideal position in goal because he himself was a goalie and remembers the pain and the humiliation of being the one the rest of the lads routinely blamed for defeat.

Favouritism kills a boys' football team, it is the thing that rots its morale quicker than a dose of paraquat. It is the natural condition of the adolescent to be convinced the world is against him. It is there in every choice of music, in every reaction to a school teacher, in every 'it's not fair'. With that prevailing mindset, there is nothing young kids can sniff out quicker than someone else getting preferential treatment. And when they do get a whiff of it, it merely confirms their sense that the world is unjust.

They know it. Know it isn't fair. It sits in their minds, festering. Not fair.

Though by no means the star player, Barney has always been worth his place in our team. Everyone can see that in his attitude, no one can point the finger. His effort is undeniable, his spirit unfettered. He has, in short, got his father off the hook on this one.

With Jeff, though, it was different. And it was hard not to sympathise.

He was an old colleague of mine. We'd worked together years back in London. He even turned out a couple of times for the Willy Wankers: not a bad player as I recall, if a little overwrought. Some of the lads had looked rather unhappy when, on only his second appearance, he gave Simon the barrister an unrestrained mouthful for not tracking back. I could tell by a couple of the looks they shot each other they thought he was taking it all a bit seriously. After all, everyone knew Simon didn't track back. That's what Simon did: he didn't track back. Actually he didn't move at all.

Soon after that game, Jeff had moved on to another paper and we'd lost touch. All we had in common was a shared workplace and football. Enough to sustain many a male relationship, I admit. But not in this case. Then one day a good ten years later, I was down at the municipal dump and I spotted him across the cardboard recycling skip. We shook hands and got talking. Turned out he'd only just moved in locally. He was downsizing, he said. Rediscovering his quality of life. He'd taken redundancy a couple of years before and had left the media altogether.

'Full of tossers,' he said. 'Waste of oxygen, the lot of them. You still in that game? I'd get shot of it if I were you. Get rid, mate. Only way. You only have one life and you're wasting yours if you carry on with that lark.'

He had family and his son was Barney's age. What's more, Jeff was looking for somewhere for the lad to play football. I told him about our team, who were then under-elevens and invited him along to training. Jeff said his boy had some talent.

'I don't want to oversell him.' he said. 'But you'll be impressed.'

They both turned up to our next session, Jeff and Jeff Junior. And Jeff stayed for the whole time. He seemed very keen. So much so, that afterwards he asked if I needed any help in the coaching department. As it happened, Barry's boy Lee had just been picked up by the local league team for their academy and Barry had just told me he wouldn't be able to come along any longer. I needed all the help I could get, so I said, sure, why not.

He wasn't shy Jeff, he soon made his feelings known. After the second training session he came to, a shambolic occasion admittedly, he stepped forward into the middle of the group at the end and told the boys that unless they were going to take all this seriously there was no point them coming along.

'You're wasting your time and more to the point you're wasting ours,' he said. Seemed a little harsh a way to address a bunch of ten-year-olds, but I said nothing.

'Who's he?' I heard Rory ask Patrice on the way out to the car park. 'Right dick.'

And that was where it all started.

As for his son, well JJ was not quite as advertised. He was a game lad, if a little uncoordinated. He could strike the ball firmly enough and during one of his first matches scored a screamer of a goal against our nearest geographical rivals. It was a goal which his father celebrated as if it were the strike that won the European Cup, rather than a consolation at the end of a drubbing in an under-tens game. After almost breaking the world static high jump record as the ball smacked into the goal, Jeff had fallen to his knees on the touchline, shut his eyes and clasped his hands together as if in thankful prayer.

'Excited man,' said Hamish, whose own exuberance suddenly paled beside this technicolour outburst.

'Very,' I said, watching the opposition's parents nudging each other and sniggering.

That celebration was a rarity, however. Most of the time, Jeff was much less happy. It was pretty obvious from the start that he invested a lot of emotion in his son. And the emotions he normally expressed were: pain, sorrow and misery. On the touchline, he suffered for and with the boy. He was not a man who had much fun at his football.

His whole focus was on the lad's game, his entire energy was consumed by it. During a game, he shouted at no one else, he watched no one else, he was interested in no one else.

We were playing seven-a-side in those days on a small pitch that abutted the main eleven-a-side field. There was very little room along that adjoining touchline – you could do little more than just stand and watch and wait till the game was over if you needed to move. JJ played either as winger or full back and Jeff would park himself on the line nearest to where the boy was positioned. He would then follow the lad up and down, often running to keep level. As he went, he issued an uninterrupted flow of instructions, constantly telling the boy what to do.

'Go on, son, work him, work him, that's it, son, now

advance, now advance, drop now, drop, work him now, work him now.'

So fiercely did he concentrate on his boy that almost every game he would collide with other spectators, or fall over the substitutes sitting on the grass, or step on the toes of the linesman. Once he ran into the set of stepladders which had been brought out from the club-house to fit the nets into the goals on the main pitch and ended up in a heap of galvanised steel. It sounded like someone had just demolished the Eiffel Tower as he tumbled, with the steps folding in over the top of him. As he scrambled and scrabbled his way out of this tempo-rary corset, it was clear his eyes had not left the action for a second.

'Give it JJ,' he shouted, as he brushed himself down.

This was his touchline mantra, soon picked up by the other boys.

'Will you give it JJ,' Rory would shout, ironically.

It was whispered under their breath by the other parents to each other.

'Know why we lost?' I'd hear one of them say to the others after we had been defeated. And they'd all chorus: 'It's because we didn't give it JJ.'

Maybe Jeff didn't hear the whispers, because it remained his major tactical input:

'Give it JJ.' That and to tell some of the less able lads that they might as well not bother showing up as they were never in a million years going to make footballers. He'd usually preface such observations by saying, 'With all due respect'. And the succinctness of his appraisal could be brutal.

'With all due respect, Rufus, you're a useless goalkeeper, always will be,' he'd say.

Or, 'With all due respect, Luke, your attitude stinks.'

Jeff was a good man at heart. He was reliable and dedicated and put in hours of work and effort. The thing is, what he wanted more than anything was for his son to be the hero, to be popular, to be the star. To score goals and win friends, to be admired by his peers. We are all like that. That is what every parent on every touch-line in the country on every single Sunday morning is hoping. This is what we all wish for as we stand there in a downpour: that our damp and grey lives will be momen-tarily brightened by our boy's prowess, that he will tackle that tackle, dribble that dribble, score that goal that we can frame in our memory as a moment of our parenting lives. And that everyone will love him.

Jeff's longing, though, was overwhelming. Such was the narrowness of his focus on JJ, I used to feel claustrophobic standing on the far touchline. As for the boy, it seemed to me that he was the least comfortable person in their own skin I had ever encountered. He could not keep still for a second. If I substituted him, from the moment he left the pitch he would be by my side, tugging my shirt asking, 'Can I go back on now? Can I go back on? When can I go back on? Now?' And if he did go back on, he would fidget and twitch and jiggle, chewing at his cuffs, forever squirming under the full-beam intensity of his father's desperation.

'How do you think I did?' he would ask as he buzzed round me after a game. 'I think I did well. I think I'll be man of the match today. My dad thinks I will be too.'

He seldom was. And when he did get the award, even as I handed it over, I could see the look in the other players' eyes. It was as if they thought he didn't deserve it. As if it was given because he'd asked and asked and asked. But mainly, it was as if they thought he got the award because his dad was one of the adults in charge. That's adults for you: wholly untrustworthy.

But now I needn't worry about that. Jeff and JJ aren't here this evening. They haven't been here for some time. Which may explain why the giggling is unabated. Mind you, the giggling increasingly seems to have one source. As I talk them through some tactics on the whiteboard in the changing room, I catch a couple of the looks that Tim shoots Gio and Gio exchanges with Faisal and Faisal gives the ceiling as he tries to stifle his snigger. I've been getting the feeling over the last few weeks that much of the laughing has a single cause. Me.

12

The committee

It is halfway through a committee meeting and we are embroiled in the intricacies of staffing the tea bar. Malcolm's daughter runs it at the moment. A kind-faced girl of fifteen, she turns up every Saturday and Sunday morning, serves tea and sweets for about three hours while matches are taking place, clears away afterwards and earns about four pounds and fifty pence for her efforts. A figure, I suspect, that is largely thanks to subsidy from her father, who helps her buy the stock at the local cash and carry. She is an uncomplaining presence about the place on matchdays, a gentle ambassador for the club. And best of all, it always means there's a cup of coffee to be had. Albeit usually lukewarm.

But Ian is not happy. He is not happy at all, he says, with the current arrangement. Nothing personal, Ian says, but he feels that the tea bar should be a source of income for the club, that the rota of parent volunteers should be re-established and that by enlarging the menu on offer, perhaps by including some organic burgers, some health snacks, some fruit teas, maybe some home-made flapjacks, the profit could be substantial.

'Surely a club like ours could be offering something better than the rubbish we are at the moment?' he says. 'Plus, don't we have a responsibility to the children in our care to offer them healthy snack choices?'

'OK, well you run it then,' says Malcolm. 'Esther's had enough anyway. Would prefer a lie-in Sundays.'

'Listen,' says Ian, 'I'm not saying Esther's not doing a reasonable enough job in a limited way. I just feel there's potentially a source of significant funds being missed here.'

'Like I said, you run it then,' says Malcolm.

'It's a philosophical question,' says Ian.

'A bloody what?' says Malcolm.

'It's a philosophical question,' says Ian.

'Really, oh, I thought it was a tea bar selling teas, coffees and light refreshments.'

'Don't be like that, you know perfectly well—'

'I'm being like that? Hang on a minute, it wasn't me who introduced the idea of philosophy into how you boil a bloody kettle.'

At this point I intervene.

'Can we move on to the next item on the agenda, gentlemen?' I say.

There is a pause for a moment before Mike, who is acting as the secretary, raises a procedural issue.

'Well, what about the last item?' he says. 'Has any decision been reached?'

'I don't know,' I say. 'Has any decision been reached?'

'No, obviously not,' says Malcolm.

'No, it hasn't,' says Ian.

'Not really, no,' I say to Mike.

'How do I minute that?' he asks.

'Put no decision reached,' I say.

'Right,' says Mike. 'Shall I just put that for everything to save time?'

'Why not?' I say. Yes, why not.

As chairman of the club I really have no idea what I am doing. I don't know procedures, I don't know about minutes, I don't know about quorums and I don't know about the club constitution. That is assuming we have one. That would be fine, except as chairman I am ultimately responsible. If the club goes bust, I have to take the rap. That's what Malcolm told me only last week.

'You're the chairman,' he said. 'If you don't get a grip, you're legally responsible.'

Yes, that's the same Malcolm who told me in the pub that evening a year or so back that my position as chairman would be entirely ceremonial and that he and Ian would do all the day-to-day administrative operations and then about a month ago sent me an email saying his working relationship with Ian had broken down to the point where, frankly, soon he couldn't be responsible for his actions.

It was obvious for some time from the atmosphere at committee meetings that the dream team pairing of Ian and Malcolm had turned into one of those nightmares that involve running naked down the aisles at your local Sainsbury's being mocked by all the members of your infant school class while your first girlfriend cavorts with your best mate in the tinned fruit section.

The thing is, they are both blokes I get along with. Individually. Malcolm is a superb coach, his age group top of the county league, while Ian is full of ideas and ambitions. For a heady six months or so after Doug left, things seemed to be moving seamlessly in the upward trajectory. We were growing, we were buzzing. When the pair first got together organising things, there used to be dozens of us at committee meetings, corralled by their emails, their phone calls, their chivvying. The two of them organised the club's most profitable summer tournament ever. Ian brought in a child protection officer, a schools liaison officer, a girls' team coordinator. He was in the process of securing FA funding for everything from new kit to a new set of goalposts for the seven-a-side pitch. He had started to send every team manager on official FA coaching courses, where they could learn the correct use of fluorescent bibs and how to place plastic cones in the shape of an octagon. For a few weeks, he even published a rota of parents to man the tea bar. Or rather woman it: they were exclusively mums. We really seemed to be getting somewhere when Malcolm made an arrangement with our local league club and we held one meeting in an executive box overlooking the pitch. We talked then of liaison with the big club, of becoming its feeder operation, of free tickets to matches, of boys and girls being matchday mascots, of their players coming to our place to run training sessions, of our boys being accepted into the academy, and of us getting first pick of any kids who dropped out. We were a club on the march.

But those looking more carefully than me would have seen the fissures in their partnership. Committee meetings were awash with undercurrents I couldn't begin to navigate. Somehow, put these two together and it was the opposite of alchemy. They soon began to argue, bicker over everything from which team should have priority for floodlit training spaces to how many portable toilets were required for the summer tournament. Nine months into my chairmanship, if Ian had told me it was Tuesday tomorrow, Malcolm would have emailed to say, no it's not, it's Wednesday. And copied everyone in who had ever had anything to do with the club, including the bloke who delivered those portable toilets and the Brazilian chap who was manager of the under-thirteens for a fortnight a few years ago until Doug sacked him for being, apparently, 'too Brazilian'. Not even Steve McClaren could make such a misfiring whole out of such promising constituent parts. And the upshot is, they have both told me in the last week or so that they no longer want to be on the committee. Life, they both tell me, is too short.

I know what they mean.

So here I am, no longer chairman in name, but chairman in fact, the last man standing. Now the two blokes who said they would be the workers, the pack mules, the sherpas on the club's steady upward march have turned back towards base camp. Soon it will be me organising the meetings, calling the council to reline the pitches, fielding phone calls from irate mothers upset that their child is not getting a fair chance in the under-tens.

The next course of action is to get a sign made and fitted to the front of my house. One that could announce to any passing charity collector, Jehovah's Witness or burly chap insisting that he is an ex-miner now trying to make a living selling oven gloves and real leather chamois at roughly four times the price of Halfords that 'a king-sized sucker lives here'.

When I get home, I tell my wife that the two of them have fallen out and that I'm being left to hold the baby, which has just soiled its nappy. A friend of hers is round, complaining about her husband. As it happens, this very week, there is some sort of crisis involving Wayne Rooney and a red card that is exercising the news. Football, it is being suggested by our more bellicose tabloid columnists, is everywhere in moral freefall.

'Told you so,' my wife says when she hears the news. 'It was always going to happen. Soon as you agreed to be chairman.'

She's right.

'What's going on?' asks her friend.

'Well,' I say. 'I've had to take on the running of our football club. There's been a bit of a crisis.'

'What?' she says, looking incredulous. 'You mean, you're taking over Manchester United?'

If only. That would be easy.

When he was in charge, Doug used to run the club like it was his own business. You wouldn't have wanted the books to be inspected too rigorously by any scrupulous authority but every year he delivered a surplus on the budget. By the time he gave up, he had built up a sizeable deposit in an internet account. He was on top of things, he was in charge, he knew what he was doing. Everyone knew he was the man who would sort things out.

Me, I'm clueless. Already people have been ringing me to ask where the stopcock is in the tea bar, or where the fusebox is for the floodlights on the hard surface, and I haven't a clue. Until now, I've just told them to ring Ian or Malcolm. But now they don't want to know any more. They have had enough of the club, of the committee, but mainly of each other.

It seems my chairmanship is not exactly going to go down in club history as a period of unfettered triumph. Tonight is the last meeting either of them will attend, they both tell me. At least they agree on something.

'Shall we move on to the next item on the agenda, gentlemen?' I say. Then I pause:

'Erm, anyone got a clue what it is?'

'With all due respect, Mr Chairman,' says Mike. 'If you don't know, who will?'

13

The tea bar

Two weeks later, Ian is back on the tea bar trail. He has called me and says he wants to know what the club's income stream is. He wants to know how come I am standing by and letting us miss out on the huge potential revenue stream there is in refreshments.

'You know Stansfield make six thousand pounds a year out of their tea bar,' he tells me.

'Are you sure?' I say. 'They're not exactly Starbucks.'

'Six thousand,' he repeats. 'Something is going on here.'

'I'm sure Esther's not—'

'I'm not suggesting any impropriety,' he says. 'Not for a moment. Just mismanagement.'

'Ian, I thought you said you were taking a back seat.'

'That doesn't seem to be a good idea right now, does it?' he says.

He then asks to see the club books.

'Sure,' I say. 'I'm all for transparency. I've got them somewhere at home. Come round and pick them up when it's convenient.'

'Today's good for me.'

When I dig them out, buried under a gathering drift of paper, I discover on the top of the file is a handwritten sheet saying, 'Annual Report.' It is in Doug's writing and consists of about six rows of numbers, alongside single words like 'Expenses' and 'Five-a-side tournament'. I gulp. Ian is picking them up in twenty minutes.

14

Who'd be a goalie?

Barney is injured again. He has a problem with his shins. The recurring problem with his shins. The one that crops up every so often and makes him walk like Douglas Bader with a limp. But he won't admit to it. He insists on soldiering on in the fond belief that, like all inconveniences, like all issues, like all parental concerns, like the washing-up, if left unattended and ignored it will just fade away. He has simple faith that, unlike Douglas, he will soon get his legs back.

And Barns isn't the only one carrying a knock. We're told that half the nation's youth is growing obese through lack of exercise, as they sit in front of their Bebo and Facebook slobbing into flabby blimps, their hands buried in skips full of nachos, their noses shoved into buckets of liquid diabetes, saturated fat glooping through their veins. Yet those who actually do something are being knackered by over-exercise; at least five of the lads are carrying stress injuries. These are fourteen-year-old boys, their bodies growing apace, their bones not yet set, their muscles stretched like piano wire. They need to rest, but the talented sportsmen in my squad are in demand from school and county, area and representative side, never mind Sunday football. Everyone wants them to turn out and they want to turn out for everyone. Which means every week Ryan hobbles along to training saying he has been clobbered in a rugby match, Paul's back has been strained by bending over a hockey stick, and Jamie and Lee are both suffering from long-term groin strains picked up in school or county games. As for Kal, his ankles are almost permanently sore. He has not lasted a full game for a year, and if he turns out for us at all these days he hobbles off after the first heavy tackle. He is our captain, our inspiration, our physical presence in an increasingly physical game and he spends most of the time standing on the touchline watching. More often than not with a bevy of fourteen-year-old girls for company, most of whom seem less interested in the flow of the game than in the sight of Tim in shorts.

Girls notwithstanding, Barney won't stand on the sidelines and watch. He may hurt, he may walk in an odd stilted roll as if he has just filled his pants, but he dares me to stop him playing.

'I'm fine,' he says, when I ask him if he's OK after seeing him this morning struggle, step by step, down the stairs.

He gets it periodically, a pain behind his shins that seizes up his muscles and makes running hurt, walking sore and hobbling the best option. He's suffered with it ever since he went to his middle school at nine. And when I say suffer, back then the torture was as much mental as physical.

In the first week at his new school there were trials for the various seven-a-side teams. The games teacher had asked them in their first PE lesson who played for a football club. Barney, Paul and Fraser all put up their hands, together with a couple of others who were signed up with other clubs hereabouts. The teacher had told them that they were as good as selected, because they knew how to play the game. The trials, he implied, would be more or less a formality.

I'd told Barney if he was going to go along to the trials he must tell the teacher beforehand that he had a problem with his shins. He said, nah, he was sure he'd be OK by Tuesday. It would have cleared up, he'd be moving fine. I told him it was best to be sure: anyway if it hurt, we didn't want to make it worse.

'All right,' he said. 'I'll tell him. But I'll be OK.'

When I turned up to collect him that Tuesday, deliberately getting there early so I could gather a few tips on how to do these things, it was immediately obvious he wasn't OK. The only way he could get mobile without hurting was to keep his legs straight. So he wobbled through it all, stiff-kneed and rigid-ankled, looking like Spotty Dog from *The Woodentops*.

'Come on Chalky boy,' I heard the teacher say as Barn stumbled through the drills and exercises, staggering round poles and cones, his legs stiff and unyielding. 'My granny's quicker than you are. And she's dead.'

Bit harsh, I thought. But then he did look ungainly.

At the end, I stood to the side with Hamish and a few other parents and watched as the teacher addressed the boys.

'Right, here's the A team. When you hear your name, you can go find your mum or dad and go home: Fraser, Paul, Will G, Will W, Tommy, Ed and, er, who else? I forgot someone . . .'

Barney stuck up his hand.

'Don't be ridiculous, Chalky. No, who is it?' he said, scanning the expectant faces. 'Ah yes, Rawding. Off you go, Rawding. Now, here's the B team.'

And again when he ran through the names, Barney's was not among them.

'And here's the Cs.'

By now, I could see Barney's head was down. When his name wasn't included even in the Cs, even among the spods and the nerds, the geeks and the ones who could barely kick a ball, I saw his nine-year-old's shoulders begin to sink.

'Right, who's left?'

Barney, several chess players, a couple of fat lads and a boy in glasses so thick they appeared to have been fashioned from the porthole of a nuclear sub, were all that remained. They put up their hands.

'Good. Well, you lot, you can help me collect all the cones and bibs.'

When we were walking back to pick up our bikes, Barney with his head down in a corrosive mix of shame and disappointment, I asked him why the teacher was so unsympathetic to an obviously injured boy. He didn't reply.

'You did tell him, didn't you?' I said, knowing how stubborn, how stoic he was.

'No,' he said.

'Why not?'

He shrugged his shoulders.

I turned round and walked back to where the teacher was putting a bag of balls into the boot of his car.

'Er, excuse me,' I said. 'Sorry, but that wasn't the real Barney out there, you know.'

He looked at me as if he had heard it all before from parents trying to excuse their boys' poor performance, trying to big up their skill, trying to fight their battles for them.

'No, really,' I said. 'He's got a problem with his shins. I'm taking him to the doctor. I think it's shin splints. Really, he's much quicker than you saw today.'

'Sure, sure,' the teacher said. 'I could see that, realised there must be a problem. I mean, he couldn't naturally be that slow, could he?'

It took him an age, but with rest the problem eased and Barney got his place in the A team for the rest of the season. A couple of years later, it came back. Same time of the year, after a long summer lay-off just as the rigour of sport kicked in once more, as soon as he started training and playing two, three, four times a week. This time rest didn't solve it as quickly and I took him back to the GP. The bloke felt his shins and told him it was just one of those things. Couldn't find a cause or offer a solution.

'A couple of ibuprofen should ease things,' he said.

That's GPs for you: just give them a pill. Even when the patient is twelve.

I thought all that was behind us now he had grown so much. If the condition was growing-related, surely he'd be over it now that he is gravel-voiced, now that his sweat glands have been switched on in a perpetual torrent, now that he is almost taller than me. Then I see him taking an age to get downstairs, a little wince on his face at every hobble.

'Barn, have you got your shins again?' I say.

'I'll be fine,' he says.

'You're hobbling.'

'Just took a knock in rugby.'

'You sure?'

'Yeah.'

'Big game today.'

'I'll be OK.'

'Sure?'

'Yeah.'

'OK.'

That's quite a lengthy conversation between us these days. Once we chatted all the time, for hours at a time, as he seemed eager for my opinion on any subject under the sun, though mostly football, asking me questions as if I had the whole *Rothmans Yearbook* in my head.

'Dad, what's the biggest crowd at a football match?'

'Dad, why do referees wear black?'

'Dad, have United ever signed a player from Altrincham?'

Actually, maybe he never asked me that. Maybe I am getting him confused with me as a kid asking my dad endless questions. Whatever, we have now reached a point where neither of us can address for long even a subject as basic as his fitness.

Mind you, at least we do converse. I remember back when I was Barney's age, my own dad and I never talked. It wasn't that we had incendiary rows or went in for door-slamming exits, it was just we never talked. The natural condition between us when we were alone together was silence. We had nowhere to meet verbally, no territory in common to spark a chat. I liked football, he liked trains; I liked David Bowie, he liked Gilbert and Sullivan; I liked Monty Python, he liked Tom Lehrer. Any exchanges we had were restricted to pleasantries and the occasional bollocking for not throwing the cat out at night.

'Who do you think will do it?' he'd say. 'Your mother?'

It is a comment I find myself making at least once a week these days.

With my dad, I remember sitting alone in the same room as him, perhaps to watch telly, and I could feel the tension rising in both of us. Physically feel it. You could hear it in our breathing, as if there was a fear between us, the fear of intimacy. I don't want to sit like that on my sofa with my boys, on one side of a widening gulf between father and son. I want to talk. I want still to be part of their lives. Thank God for the football, then. At least it provides one place where we meet on some sort of common ground. At least it provides some sort of intimacy, even an ersatz one.

So I try again later in the morning as we make our way to the game.

'Where do you want to play today?'

'Don't mind.'

'You could go midfield if Paul and Kal are still out.'

'Sure. Wherever.'

'But you'll be OK, leg-wise?'

'Fine.'

'Sure?'

'Yeah, no problem.'

I guess that counts as a pre-match fitness test.

It is one of those days that almost give winter a good name. At the end of a week of unyielding grey, in which sky and townscape have merged into a uniform murk, in which a scud of damp and grime has coated every pavement, doused every building, Sunday dawns suddenly with a full palette of colour. The sun shines, the air is sharp, it is the sort of day when you want to wrap a scarf round your neck, put on a duffel coat and kick your way through the piles of reddened leaves banked up on the side of the road. Except were you to do so round our way, you'd be certain to step in a hidden deposit and end up with it all over your shoes.

The parental supporters, the loyal band of dads, mums, stepdads and same-sex life partners, turn up full of chat and smiles, happy that this week at least they will not be returning home after the match with trousers as wet as Llandudno, and the beginnings of pneumonia lurking at the back of their throats. I gather the team together. We are on the march, I say. Even if we are without Paul, Kal, Ryan and Lee, I tell them, we cannot fail. The momentum belongs to us now, I say.

Thirty minutes later, the momentum has evaporated. We are four goals down. It is not the fault of Barney's fitness. He has been moving around gamely, if not quite as quickly as normal, his teeth gritted as he runs through the midfield, straining to intercept the ball. It is not the fault of Tim or Fraser or Franz or Jamie who have been battling in the absence of their injured team-mates till the sweat pours down their faces. It is not the fault of the bevy of girl supporters, who cheer Tim's every touch.

'One Tim Jackson, there's only one Tim Jackson, one Timmy Jaa-aa-ckson!'

No, all four goals have but a single cause: the goal-keeper. While everyone else turned up happy and smiling, Max arrived this morning looking edgy. I asked him if he was OK and of course he said he was fine. That's what fourteen-year-old boys do. So I asked Barry to warm him up separately from the rest of the team and as I watched him leaping and bouncing and catching the balls Bazz chucked at him, I thought I could see the confidence seeping back. He'll be fine, Bazz had said. And I thought, He is such a nice lad, he deserves to be.

But then, as soon as the match starts, he begins to run through the whole range of custodial cock-ups. If Baddiel and Skinner still made videos of comedy football howlers, they could fill half the tape with this morning. He has miskicked a back pass straight to their forward; he has let a long shot slip through his hands; he has dived over a mishit slice; and he has slipped as he goes to gather another back pass, somehow managing as he does so to scoop the ball over the line. What Fabien Barthez, René Higuita and all those other flaky eccentrics managed across a career, Max achieves in less than half a game. The poor lad: so exposed, so vulnerable, he stands there, his head down, his hands hanging by the side of him, limp. He is the broken keeper. In front of him, the opposition cackle about the pitch as their coach shouts:

'Come on, lads, the keeper's a joke, shoot from anywhere.'

The last thing the boy needs is to be blamed by his own team, he knows what he has done. I don't want the boys to take an accusatory lead from me. So I stand on the touchline in silence. Alongside me, Barry shouts, 'Chin up, Max', and 'Could happen to anyone, mate', at him a couple of times, but we all know there is no way back from this. Rory's father, approaches me:

'You've got to do something. I told you we had a problem there a couple of weeks back. He looks terrified.'

I nod.

'Put Rory in goal,' he says. 'He won't let you down.'

'Rory? I thought he always wanted to play up front.'

'He does,' he says. 'But anything is better than this. Come on.'

It isn't over. There is time before the interval for more.

Just after Rory has pulled a goal back, they score again. And this time it is Barney's fault. In a goalmouth scramble, he has a chance to clear but – perhaps because his legs aren't functioning properly, perhaps because he thought the goalie might get it, perhaps because he was thinking too much – he hesitates, just for a moment pausing to get his balance instead of slamming his foot through the ball. Their centre forward, a big, bustling, barging oaf of a boy, pushes across him and then smacks the ball past Max, who by now has no mental strength left even to make a token effort at saving it and just stands, rooted to his line, arms by his side.

Barney's is the kind of mistake that infects defences when the goalkeeper is absent. Panic pours through them: you can see the confidence disappearing from every sinew, uncertainty is everywhere. For years it's been like this: we could have been contenders had we had someone between the posts with the authority to domi-nate. I thought Max might be the answer, but Rory's dad is right. It has been clear for some time his nerves are getting in the way. Today, he looks lost between the posts, tiny in his big shirt, the sleeves hanging over his hands. Today the boy who saved that penalty a couple of weeks back is but a distant, thin memory. Today he is suffering.

But it is not him I publicly blame. Not him I shout at. The frustration, the anger, the humiliation of watching us sink only bursts to the surface when Barn makes his error. After watching Max's howlers in silence, it all now comes out. I give my own son such a mouthful from the touchline, even I am taken aback by its force.

'What the bloody hell are you doing, boy? Clear the bloody thing when you get the chance,' I yell.

And even as I shout, I regret it. What am I doing? Is this really how I want to communicate with my son, by screaming abuse at him? Is this really the route to intimacy, to trust, to friendship? He looks at me, so hurt, so disappointed, so let down. For a moment I can see him thinking about replying. It would be legitimate just to bawl back: 'What the hell are you shouting at me for? It's bloody him you should be yelling at.' Nobody would have blamed him had he done so. But he is too much of a team player, not to mention too kind a person, to apply the final boot to what is left of Max's confidence. He looks at Max, looks back at me and shakes his head. It is a response that is eloquence itself, that moment of restraint demonstrating that he is already a better man than I'll ever be. It shuts me up instantly.

A couple of minutes later as he comes over to the touchline to take a throw-in I say quietly, 'Sorry, Barn.'

He looks back at me and shrugs.

'It's OK.'

But I'm not sure it is.

As the half-time whistle blows, Max sinks to his knees, buries his face in his hands and sobs. Tim puts his arm round him and tells him he is a brilliant keeper and a top mate. A motivational guru could not have scripted a better response. These boys, how do they know how to say just the right thing? They're just fourteen, yet their instinctive reading of psychology is way more sophisticated than most adults of my acquaintance. It's certainly better than mine. Tim helps him to his feet and the two of them join the rest of the boys gathering round me. They all stand in nervy quiet, Max's snuffling the loudest noise. They look quickly one to the other but say nothing. Max stands head down. Everyone knows what is going on, yet it remains unspoken. It has to. There is no point saying anything. I break the silence.

'Bad luck, Max, not your day, mate,' I say quickly. 'Rory, you go in goal in the second half.'

It is like releasing a valve. As everyone claps him on the back and says, 'Unlucky, mate', what is left of the air in Max's body seems to seep away. He walks over to the fence running along the touchline, sinks to the turf, brings his knees up to his chest and cries the sort of gulping, chest-heaving tears that, if his mother had been there to see them, would have made her heart break. Thank heavens she isn't: she would have had a good case to prosecute. Meanwhile, I can hear drifting across the pitch the opposition giggling about how crap the goalkeeper is. God, this is a harsh game, I think.

Then I tell Rory to concentrate and keep talking and get the ball out to the wide men as soon as he gathers it.

A couple of days later I am at Manchester United's Carrington training centre to interview Brian McClair, the club's former centre forward, who is now head of the youth academy. I am here to write a piece on United's revolutionary approach to developing their young prospects, but I have only one question running through my mind as I drive up the motorway, through the suburbs west of Manchester and out into scrubby, semi-industrial countryside: the goalkeeper question.

United's Carrington base is next to an oil refinery, beside a lorry depot, at the end of a long straight lane. Access is controlled by a security barrier. Alongside the barrier is a discreet sign telling visitors that players should not be pestered for autographs as they will not sign them due to unauthorised trading. Standing by the sign are half a dozen men in United anoraks and tracksuits, holding carrier bags, waiting to pester the players for autographs. The bloke nearest the barrier peers into my car as I push the security intercom.

''S a'right, lads,' he tells the rest of the group. 'He's nobody.'

It looks, when you have gained access to the centre, as if you have taken a wrong turning and ended up in a hi-tech business park, filled as it is with low-rise steel and glass pavilions, softly tinkling fountains and freshly planted shrubbery. It is, perhaps, the HQ of a software production company, or a global pharmaceutical giant. Only the arrival in a minibus of a dozen burly youths, who walk through the car park to the front door with the easy, bow-legged swagger of those who know they are special, gives the game away, lets you know that the product being conceived here is not computers or painkillers but footballers.

The reception looks like a sleek boutique hotel, all marble and glass and leather upholstery. Although not many boutique hotels have scenes from Manchester United history on the wall, colour prints of goal celebrations and trophies being lifted. Nor do many boutique hotels have Ji-Sung Park emerging from a side room clutching a couple of tickets for Saturday's game.

'Hope they enjoy it, Sunny,' a voice calls from within the room.

'Ah, very nice, good,' says the Korean international, bowing as he leaves.

The woman behind reception is astonishingly informal and friendly.

'Brian, love, there's someone in reception for you,' she says when she calls McClair on her phone.

'He won't be a minute, love,' she says to me. 'Fancy a brew?'

When he emerges, McClair too is just as friendly, striding out of his office to greet me with a smile and an extended hand.

'A'right, mate,' he says. 'Have you got a brew?'

Blimey, I think, what a nice bloke; I hope he doesn't recognise my voice as the one which once in the early nineties emerged from the Stretford End suggesting that he was a useless tosser who couldn't hit a cow's arse with a banjo.

Alongside his team of coaches, McClair has been charged by the United senior management with a ten-year plan of producing an entire first team of academy graduates. It is a task which consumes his every waking moment: developing strategies, thinking of better systems, working out new methodologies. Put a tape recorder on him and within a couple of hours you have a blueprint of how to school young footballers. And when I tell him that I coach Barney's team, he becomes, if anything even more enthused.

'Well, you'll know this stuff,' he says occasionally. Also: 'Stop me if I'm telling you stuff you already know.'

We talk and talk, but there is one thing I need to find out from him urgently.

'Can I ask you something about my team?'

'Sure,' he says. 'Fire away.'

And I ask him: what would he advise me to tell the lads, who have just lost a game they might have won because of keeper error?

'We have it here,' he says. 'That's the first thing to remember, goalies make mistakes at every level. The point is this: everyone celebrates a goal. It's not just the scorer, everyone joins in. Everyone feels chuffed to be part of it. Equally, when you let a goal in, everyone has to take responsibility. Maybe the kid who had a shot when he shouldn't have done and you go on to lose possession and that led to a goal. Or maybe the kid who didn't make the tackle in midfield, or who didn't track back with the runners. We're all in this together. But it's the goalie who's most exposed. He's the one it's easy to blame when maybe it was never his fault at all. I just say to the lads: next week he'll make three blinding saves that will keep you in a game you deserve to lose.'

The important thing, he adds, is to make a public statement of support for your keeper. And to make sure everyone buys into it.

Good advice. At the next training session, I try it. After Barry has conducted the warm-up, I call the boys into the centre circle and tell them they didn't deserve to lose on Sunday and that mistakes can happen to anyone. I tell them that they all celebrate when someone scores a goal, so they need to take collective responsibility for any they concede. I tell them that though the goalie made a mistake last week, next week he might well make three blinding saves that will allow us to win a game we deserve to lose. Next week, I say, the goalie will get us out of trouble.

It sounds good as I say it. But the problem is, Max isn't here tonight to hear it. Nobody knows where he is. He didn't say anything at school to the other lads about not coming. He just hasn't shown up, so I can't give him that public vote of confidence. And in his absence, I hear Gio whisper, loudly enough for most of the rest of the lads to catch it: 'Max get us out of trouble? You're having a laugh.'

15

Who is it for?

As we sit in the Carrington complex, Brian McClair gives
me a simple bit of advice.

'Football', he says, 'is its own best teacher.'

The best way to coach young players, he adds, is to let
them play as much football as possible. Don't be distracted
by peripherals, don't be diverted by tangential ideas, don't
spend too long on the internet looking for complicated
drills involving cones and bibs, don't lecture for hours on
end about formations while standing in front of the chalk-
board. Chuck them a football and just let them play.

'In my job, you're always trying to find ways to give
the kids an edge,' he says. 'I remember once going to an
international tournament and noticing that young
Brazilian kids seem to be lighter on their feet, more flexible, more agile; they don't fall down in heaps, they bounce
over tackles, skip through them. When we got back, we
started to look at ways to improve our players in that
field. Could we get someone in to work on their balance,
give them exercises? We have an eye specialist here who
helps with their vision. We thought about the way we

were brought up and what we used to do and wondered if that had something in it, maybe if they climbed trees and jumped out of them it would give them useful physical skills. But you can't have a person full-time teaching them how to climb trees. The pressure's on time: we've only got a finite amount of it. Anyway, I always quote Paul Scholes as an example. People all through his career said, hey, what a player he would be with an extra yard of pace. But I say this: Scholes with another yard of place wouldn't be the player he is. He compensated and became a fantastic football player as a result. Now he learned that playing football. Let them play football.'

The thing is, he tells me, in the past, kids played a lot more. Not in clubs or academies, but in parks and the street. What has gone from our society, he adds, is the endless amounts of informal football that very young kids used to play, the kickabouts that instilled in them a bedrock education in the game. Although some might argue simply playing a lot of street football does not necessarily turn you into Johan Cruyff, he has a point. I remember myself spending half my life as a kid going down to the local rec and playing football. Sometimes it was just one-a-side, me against Joe Noar. And even when we didn't make it to the park, we'd play wall-y for hours on end, Joe and I. We would kick the ball in turn against a wall behind my house all morning: bang, bang, bang. And then come back after lunch: bang, bang, bang, the relentless rhythm of it. McClair is undoubtedly right, there is no better teacher when it comes to trapping a ball than just kicking it for hours at a time. Shame I was such a lousy student.

And shame Barney never does that: he's good enough for it to make a difference. But for him and his mates, there are no pick-up games in the park, no wall-y, no

aimless hours in the street, kicking a ball. When we next
meet and I ask the lads how many of them go anywhere
near a football when they're not in a match or training,
I get blank looks. Modern kids don't play informal football anymore. It is not just the rival distractions of
Gameboy and the internet; parents don't like their offspring
to be out of their control, in danger from traffic and the
other predatory possibilities of modern life. People of my
generation share a dreadful culpability: we interfere way
too much in our children's lives, try to formalise their
play time, procedurise it, professionalise it. So these days,
if kids play football at all, they do so at clubs where
coaches help them with tactics and positional awareness.
But it means they have none of the experience forged
by the endless repetition of informal play. Such is progress.

'If you want to get all sociological about it, great footballers tend to emerge from poverty,' McClair tells me.
'In wealthy parts of the world, for whatever reason and
many of them good, kids don't play enough.'

That is why, he reckons, managers like Arsène Wenger
prefer to recruit young players from Africa and South
America: these are kids who arrive at sixteen having spent
hours and hours solidifying their technique through practice on the street. Of modern English players, Wayne
Rooney is rare in that he had the kind of background
conducive to developing those skills. And that is why,
McClair says, the best form of training is just to play lots
of football. To prove it, he invites me along to a session
at Carrington to see for myself. We set a date when the
United under-fourteens will be training, and I ask him if
he minds if Barry comes with me.

'No worries,' says McClair. 'See you both then.'

★   ★   ★

I get a call the day before we are due to go to Carrington from McClair. He has been called away to look at a player. But no problem, he says, we'll be in safe hands. He has asked a colleague to look after us. Barry and I speculate on the way to Manchester who will be there in McClair's stead. We fantasise it will be the big man himself, and that we will be shown round Carrington by an avuncular Sir Alex, keen to tell us the inside secrets of twenty years at United. He will be our guide through an indoor training session; he will buy us a cuppa in the canteen; he will pick our brains about how we coach the Northmeadow lads, anxious to see if he can learn anything he could put into practice with Giggsy, Scholesy and Wazza.

'Aye,' he'll say as we leave. 'And if youse two ever fancy a change of direction, you'd be welcome to a job here.'

It is no great surprise, when we roll into the car park and head for the reception, to discover that His Fergieness has something better to do with his time tonight than meet us. In McClair's stead is a tall, energetic chap with the strangest accent I have ever heard. When we meet him, Rene Mulensteen is United's skills development officer. Later he is set to join Brøndby, the Danish club, as manager. But when we turn up, he is totally absorbed in the United system and how to make its graduates more skilful footballers. A Dutchman who learned his coaching trade at Ajax, he has been in the north-west for five years and has developed a way of speaking that makes him sound like the bastard vocal love-child of Ruud Gullit and Liam Gallagher. One minute he is telling us that 'there wash a schkills schortage at this club also', the next he is saying of Barry's decision to plump for a black tea, 'no milk in your brew is it Bazz, mate? Sound.'

Mulensteen takes us across the car park into a building

that looks like a modern airport terminal. Except, as he leads us up stairs and along corridors, cheerfully first-naming everyone he meets, slapping backs and ruffling hair, there is not a Starbucks or a Body Shop or a policeman with a sub-machine gun in sight. When he opens the final door, it is as if to a magic kingdom. We find ourselves standing on a viewing gallery running high above one side of a full-sized football pitch. A state-of-the-art, artificially turfed acre of football pitch is laid out before us. There are no worries about the weather in this particular part of Manchester. Outside the December rain slants down as if from a perpetually engaged sprinkler system. But here inside conditions are dry, warm, perfect.

On the walls of the gallery are framed pictures of past members of United's youth system. There's the 1992 Youth Cup winners, now footballing celebrities, then in their acned adolescence, a side that includes the future captains of England, Wales and United. There's Mark Hughes pictured as a seventeen-year-old in a wild busby of hair and shorts so small and tight he looks as though his entire wardrobe had been chucked into the boil wash cycle. In the picture he is standing alongside Norman Whiteside, who already looks about thirty. And down on the pitch are the next generation of would-be heroes, the club's current under-fourteens, Barney's sporting contemporaries.

Though, as Jeff might say, with all due respect, you wouldn't know it. Any relation to a training session I might conduct is purely coincidental. Boy, are these fantastic footballers. They have split the pitch into two and are playing two small-sided games. So good are they as they roll their foot over the ball like Zidane, dip their shoulders like Matthews and lollipop like Ronaldo, it is impossible to work out which foot they favour. Shots, crosses, chips and passes are executed by left or right boot with equal facility. Also, so comfortable in possession is every boy, so good on the ball, so sharp in finishing, there is no telling who is a defender, who a forward. At one point, one player receives a pass, kills it on his instep, then strides forward, jinking his way up the field, beating two men as he goes before spinning a twenty yard pass out on to the toes of his winger. And he is one of the goal-keepers. This is total football, a Brazilian carnival of skill Manc-style, conducted by a bunch of boys who, in another life, might be out there asking if they might 'mind yer car, mister'.

Barry and I look at each other and shake our heads: this is the Everest of junior football and we are engaged in the foothills of the Pennines.

As the players go about their business, the coaches stand off, watching, studying, learning, but rarely intervening. The only noise you hear is the cries of 'look left' or 'square ball' emanating from the lads themselves. Not once does a coach shout – as I do all the time with my lads – instructions or suggestions. Up in the gallery, too, the parents watch in silence, not even calling out their encour-agement.

'Coaches create the environment, the boys are the ones to make the decisions,' says Mulensteen. 'So you stand back and observe. You don't interrupt constantly. Anything that comes out from the kids themselves is always better, it sticks in the mind, it is self-learning. If I say, "No, hold on, Tommy, you should have passed there", then is he aware of why he is doing it? No, it becomes your decision-making on the pitch, not his.'

The self-learning theme is there in the drills the boys

do. Their routine is based round lots of small-sided matches, each with different aims. Some are about simply dribbling the ball over a line, others are about shooting through multiple goals, others straightforward matches, but without goalkeepers. Most of them are four against four. It is the magic number, Mulensteen says, on which every passing formation in football is based: a triangle and a spare man. The passing and movement the boys will discover for themselves in such exercises become the basis of their strategy once they progress to full-scale matches. It also means that the boys have the ball at their feet far more often than in structured exercises or eleven-a-side drills.

Yet even all this is never enough. The boys are with United three times a week, for two training sessions and a match. Astonishingly for a club driven by a man as competitive as Ferguson, United are anxious to withdraw from the competitive games structure demanded by the FA academies for their younger players. The matches, the coaches say, produce an overheated atmosphere that is not good for learning. Far better to use the time to work on the three Ps: practice, practice and practice.

'We played another academy recently and our goalkeeper got injured in a challenge,' McClair tells me when I speak to him later. 'It wasn't a foul, one of those things. But we didn't have a reserve keeper on the bench. They did. And we asked if he could play for us. Now instead of saying, OK, sure, give him a game, they refused. We had to put an outfield player in goal while their reserve keeper is sat on the bench doing nothing. And then their coach was giving it all this: "Put the keeper under pressure", "He's not a keeper, have a shot." And you thought, Who is this for? The boys? Or the coach and his ego?'

That is the question that defines kids' football at every

level, even, it seems, at the top: who is it for? It is the question that runs through every coaching session, every game, every committee meeting, every dispute about the tea bar. It is the question that should be asked by every parent who has ever disputed a linesman's flag, or every coach who has left a kid on the touchline all game, an unused substitute. It is the question I don't ask myself often enough. Who is it for?

16

It's a matter of class

One thing, though, perplexes me as I make my way to the car after the Carrington training session. By day the space in front of the pitches and offices here is crammed with the Bentleys and Hummers of football's bling class. But even by night, when the first team has long gone and the only vehicles are driven by the mums and dads of the academy kids, the car park is almost full. The fact is, it would be impossible to get to this place, lying as it does up an unmarked lane in the middle of nowhere, without being driven there by someone.

'Parental support is massive,' McClair tells me. 'I'd go so far as to say you won't make it without parents. In any sport. I've spoken to people who've said: "That kid'll play for England at rugby, cricket, whatever." And I say: "Were his mum and dad at the game?" And they say: "No." And I say: "Are they ever there?" They say: "No, not really." And I come back a year later, and the kid's not there.'

He is right. This is the paradox at the heart of youth football: it may be all about the kids, but it is the parents who matter.

A few years ago, I played in a charity football match in a prison. The game was celebrities against inmates, though my very presence on the celebrity side suggested that its provenance was slightly exaggerated. It was basically a couple of actors from the RSC, a theatre director, a bunch of students and me against a team of convicts.

When the game kicked off, it was immediately obvious we were in danger of being outclassed. Luvvies against Lags: it was no contest. Up front for the inmates was a player of astonishing skill. He was twenty-one, a slight, reedy looking lad in a beanie hat. When he got the ball at his feet, he didn't run through our defence, he danced: no other description does justice to the way he moved, with such rhythm, with such balance. After I had seen him slip by our back line for about the fourth time I decided to nail him, just to show the prisoners we weren't a pushover. I'd go in for a full-scale hit, aiming with surgical precision at his ankles. I was determined to trip him, send him into orbit. The next time he got the ball and made his quicksilver way into my area of the pitch, I slid in and caught him all right, hitting him at full tilt just where I intended.

'Got him,' I thought.

But instead of him flying through the air, my shameless assault barely altered his trajectory. Such was his balance, he wobbled slightly, imperceptibly, but almost immediately recovered and strode on towards the goal. I got up from my slide and watched him head away, feeling like Ron 'Chopper' Harris must have done when he went in all studs showing against George Best and never got near him. As he ran off goalwards, I could read nothing but disdain in the shape of his back.

After the game, after the lad had scored four times and

the warder in charge had taken him off for fear of him humiliating us, I sought him out. In part, I wanted to apologise, but as we started talking, I realised there was nothing to apologise for. It would have been like a gnat seeking out a stallion to say sorry for biting his leg: he hadn't noticed.

'Surely,' I said to him, 'you must have been a pro.'

'Me?' he said. 'A pro? Nah.'

And he told me his story. He had been the best player in his neighbourhood, every coach of every boys' team in a thirty-mile radius of his home had wanted him to play for them. He came from a single-parent family and his mum didn't have a car, but it didn't matter, these coaches were prepared to pick him up for training and matches. But they were all over him, these guys, way too pushy, put too much pressure on him and he didn't like that, so he dropped out of teams, preferring to play with his mates around the estate. Even so, word seeped out and scouts from professional clubs were soon on his case. He was not naturally inclined to being noticed, no one at home was encouraging him to take their interest seriously, so he just let their advances go and got on with his life. When he was twelve, though, he was invited to a trial with Arsenal, the team he supported. This was the one, he thought, even if his mum just shrugged when he told her and said that he'd have to find his own bus money to get there. He was on his way to the trial, heading for the bus stop, boots in hand, when he bumped into some older lads from the estate.

'Where you off?' they asked. He told them. They said that they were on their way to rob a house, which would be a lot more fun. So he sacked off the trial and went with them. He found he was a good burglar, he had a knack for it. And he got well known for it too. So well that on the day of his fourteenth birthday the police came round to his flat and arrested him. Thus began an association with institutions that lasted throughout his teenage life. By the time we played in that match, he had spent no more than eighteen months of the previous seven years on the outside. Not much time for football. He was now serving a seven-year stretch for aggravated burglary. He'd be twenty-three when he got out. Minimum.

'I might give the football another go then,' he said. 'But, you know, I'll probably be too old.'

He was a contemporary of Beckham's and, on the limited evidence I had seen, maybe a more talented foot-baller. But he was a million miles from making it, now his only platform was the prison yard. It had always been like that: there was no way he would make it. And it was all down to upbringing. He was adrift as a kid, while Beckham was grounded. Beckham's old man, Ted, has seen every game his son has ever played. He was always there for him. This bloke had no one. No one at all.

So in a sense, Brian McClair had a problem with class. Sure, the best footballers might be found in the poorest backgrounds, but the system he presides over insists that those who make it to the top aren't from there. Ted Beckham was a self-employed electrician; his son might not have been born with a silver spoon in his mouth but there was plenty of cutlery rattling around in his kitchen. At United, McClair requires the young players to attend sessions at Carrington a minimum of three times a week. Even if their parents haven't got a car to drive them, then, to be successful, to make it through that system, requires someone to make sure they are ready to be picked up at the right place at the right time. It needs someone to be behind them, to be pushing them. It requires someone to be aspirational on their behalf. And the fact is, most of the parents watching the training session I saw did not look as though they were worrying where the next meal was coming from. They were well dressed, with 4×4s out in the car park. It is not just in the stands that football is rapidly becoming a pursuit of the middle classes.

It is the same even at the level I operate. When our lads were twelve, a boy turned up one time at training who was from a refugee family. Abdul was a lovely kid, smiley and polite and not a bad footballer. He lived with his mother and five brothers in a hard-to-let house on a rundown estate in the roughest part of town. It was a long distance − geographically and socially − from where we play. His mum had no means of getting him to games or training. But I didn't mind picking him up and when I couldn't make it, I'd arrange for someone else to do so.

Over the course of about a year, however, the arrangements became increasingly flaky. He wouldn't be there to be picked up, his mum had no idea where he was, or she would be working and there'd be no one at the house. When things did work out, he was a great addition to the team: lively, quick, bright. And when he did turn up, I'd try to pin down the next set of arrangements. But he was twelve years old, they'd go in one ear and straight out the other. His mum had other things on her mind, like trying to keep a young family together on her own, with her husband back in their war-torn country and her earning subsistence wages as a contract cleaner at the local hospital. It wasn't long before the gaps between him turning out became longer and longer. There was no way of contacting him except by turning up at his house before every training session or match and more often than not there would be no one there.

Then one day, he was there, I took him to training and on the way back home, he told me he wanted to go and play for another team. I was really pissed off: after all I'd done for him, I thought. Pathetic, looking back on it: all I'd actually done was pick him up and drive him home a few times. I wasn't exactly the Mother Teresa of kids' football. But at the time I thought, Sod you, then. Barney was more philosophical about it.

'Ah well,' he said. 'At least we don't have to drive miles before training every week and then find he's not there.'

A few months later, at the start of the next season, Abdul turned up at training. He came on a bike. He wanted to join us again, he said. He didn't much like the other team he'd left us for. It had been a mistake to leave.

'Brilliant,' I said, guilty that I had been so mean about his original departure. 'You're in. You're more than welcome, mate.'

After training, I arranged to pick him up that Sunday morning for a preseason friendly. Barney and I got in the car, drove out to his estate, parked outside his house, knocked on the door and no one answered. If he was there, he wasn't coming out. I pushed a note through the door saying come down to the next training session. I never saw him again.

17

The kettle

There is a crisis in the committee. During his audit of the club finances, which, judging by his emails, he concluded at midnight on Christmas Eve, Ian has discovered that, just before the last five-a-side tournament, Malcolm spent thirty-five pounds on a new catering-sized kettle for the tea bar, without first seeking the authorisation of the rest of the committee. It is, Ian says in a flurry of communication over the ether, not on. He is demanding that Malcolm be made to resign his membership of the club. He has circulated a proposal by email, provoking a lengthy response from Malcolm which, among other things, calls him 'bonkers'. Ian has subsequently threatened to consult his solicitor. Like Alsace-Lorraine or the Golan Heights, our tea bar appears to have the capacity to provoke unending conflict. And still the coffee is lukewarm.

18

Lose some, draw some

I have arrived early at the ground, waiting for the lads to turn up, waiting for the action to start. It is early February and it looks as though the colour has ebbed out of the place, seeping away on the drizzle. The trees in the little copse between the two pitches are leafless sticks, framed in damp, dripping. The weather has been like this for what seems like months: not cold, not ferocious, just pointless. I don't think I have seen any of our supporters' faces for weeks; they have all been hidden beneath hoods pulled tight and close against the continuous squall. Even Hamish seems to have gone into his shell in this weather, which takes some doing. And Luke's dad hasn't been seen at all since Christmas. I assumed it was because he didn't fancy the weather. But I bumped into him at Marks and Spencer and he said he had been banned from the touchline.

'Banned?' I said.

'Yeah,' he says.

'Why? Is it a bad luck thing or something?'

'No,' he says. 'I'm too embarrassing, apparently. My very presence is embarrassing.'

On the pitch things have now settled into a pattern. In the league, we lose some, we draw some. But in the county cup we can't stop winning. Today, after yet another win two weeks ago, we are in the quarter-final. As the luck of the draw would have it, we are at home to our nearest geographical rivals, a derby in which half of each team go to the same school. So there's a bit of edge during the week, the lads tell me. We have never done as well as this in our time together, never got so far. And I'm awash with nerves, a rip tide of worry swishes through my stomach as I stand there, wondering why on earth I came here so early.

To calm myself down, I wander over to the seven-a-side pitch where the under-eights are playing. It is a nostalgia trip, really, a journey back to the time when none of my players had facial hair, when there were no teenage girl supporters on the touchline, when tackles did not resemble a collision between two speeding HGVs. They look so tiny, these seven- and eight-year-olds, as they scurry around, falling over, bouncing back up. There appears to be no pattern to their play, just a harem-scarem dash in pursuit of the ball, a little group of them chasing it, hacking at it, failing to master it, while a few others stand apart and watch. The pattern is so haphazard, so random, so jaunty I can't help smiling. It looks carefree, fun, a giggle.

Except nobody on the touchline is giggling. Nobody is smiling. The faces framing the pitch are tight, tense, twitchy. Utterly absorbed in something that, to the outsider, looks utterly trivial.

They are just like me, then.

I learn from one of the spectators that this is a top of the table clash and that the score is even and that there are only a few minutes left.

'Big game,' he says. 'Big, big game. Whole league could depend on it.'

'I thought you just played friendlies at this stage.'

'Friendly league,' he says.

'What's that mean? Non-competitive?'

'Supposedly. But you try telling them that,' the man says.

'The kids?'

'No, them. The parents.'

He's right. There is not much friendly about these faces, or non-competitive about their attitude.

On the far side, the coach of one of the teams is bawling non-stop instructions.

'Stay back, keep it tight, stick with him.'

Next to him, another man is issuing an equally loud, equally insistent string of diametrically opposed directions.

'Push up, play it wide, lose him.'

I assume they must be the two rival coaches. But when they both stop for a moment and move towards each other to discuss a substitution, I realise they are in charge of the same team. No wonder there is no pattern to the play.

The several coaches are by no means alone in yelling. All round the pitch people are shouting. Not just 'come on, boys' or 'get stuck in' but a cacophony of tactical advice.

'Move forward, Callum,' I hear one father shout at a boy who is standing alone in his half as play buzzes round the penalty area up the other end of the pitch.

'He told me to stay back,' the boy shouts, pointing at his coach.

'Never mind that,' says the father. 'Get in there. You'll never score from there, will you?'

As the boy heads forward, his coach spots him and yells from the far side:

'Where the hell are you going, Callum? I told you to stay back.'

The boy looks imploringly at his father, who simply shrugs. A couple of moments later, when the play catches up with him, the ball lands at Callum's feet. But he is not sure what to do with it, is easily dispossessed and makes only a thin effort to win it back. Watching him lose possession so tamely, his father steps forward over the touchline and, real menace in his voice, jabs an accusatory finger in his direction:

'Do that again and you'll get it when you get home.'

The boy stops and looks at his feet.

'And don't cry, you fucking girl,' hisses his father. 'Show me you're a man for once.'

Paul Elliott, the former Chelsea and Celtic player, once told me he found it really hard to watch his son play football because of the other parents screaming and carrying on. He said most professionals and ex-pros felt the same: they couldn't believe the pressure that was exerted. Mind you, I once saw a former Premiership player at a summer youth tournament, standing on the touchline stripped to the waist, a bottle of beer in one hand, swearing at his son. It's a disease that can afflict anyone.

Of either gender. In this crowd, the mothers, if anything, are even more insistent. There is a group of three of them standing just to the side of one of the goals, a little coven of squawking and shrieking. They shout non-stop at everything and everyone: their sons, the opposition, the referee, the opposition supporters, even their own coach.

'Why encha put Ryan back on?' one of them yells.

'In a minute, in a minute,' the coach replies, keeping his gaze fixed on the game, hoping that if he ignores her she'll go away. She doesn't.

'Well, there ent that long to go. Do you wanna win it or what?'

'In a minute, in a minute,' he says, flapping his hand at her dismissively. 'Just let the others have a chance, OK.'

She turns to her friends and asks, loudly enough for no one to miss a word:

'How come it's like this every bleeding week? He's got Rhys out there, he's got Connor, he's even got bleedin' Callum. Look at him, how we gonna win it with him on?'

She shouts again.

'Get Callum off, get Ryan on.'

Callum's father, further down the line, shoots her a look.

'Steady on, Lorn,' he says.

'Oh come on, Steve,' she shouts back. 'No disrespect, but we ent gonna win fuck all with Callum on is we?'

Poor Callum, his head switching between the shouts, his concentration drifting away from the game in hand, has now given up completely. He goes nowhere near the ball for the rest of the match.

I think back to the atmosphere of studious silence that permeates the United academy and it all makes sense: how can anyone improve, better themselves, have a chance in this mayhem? How can kids enjoy the game if their parents are bickering on the touchline during a match in a league that is not even meant to be competitive? Mind you, according to Brian McClair, even at the top, where the education of parents is given almost as high a priority as the education of their sons, sanity by no means prevails. When I said to him that he was lucky to be able to conduct his coaching without pressure from parents, he laughed.

'It's not always how we'd like it when we play competitive games, believe you me,' he said. 'You'd be amazed
how many of our rivals out there want to win at all costs.
Especially against us. Even with ten-, eleven-year-olds, they
see the badge on our shirts and the parents are telling
them to go for it hell for leather. Mad sometimes. There
have been instances where we've had to get abusive parents
removed from the building. We had one chucked out the
other day. It was ridiculous what was going on. You couldn't
believe it.'

I could. What is going on here in this under-eights
game is mad enough. The whistle has blown, the result is
a draw, the coaches have slapped each other on the back
and told each other they 'have a nice little side there'.
Someone has even shouted, as they always do at the end
of a kids' football game, 'shake hands, boys'. A couple of
home supporters have started to dismantle the goals; another
is collecting the corner flags. It might have the appearance of being over, but this contest is nowhere near being
ended. The members of the coven have surrounded their
team's coach. One of them, the shouty one who wanted
to see her Ryan out on the pitch, is particularly exercised.

'It's the same every fucking week,' she says to the coach.
'I told you, get Ryan on. You don't know what you're
fucking doing, do you? Not a fucking clue.'

'He'd been on, he'd played most of the game,' the coach
replies, busying himself to avoid eye contact.

'Yeah, but you took him off for that nonce, Callum.'

'I'm just trying to give everyone a chance.'

'Give everyone a chance? What's that all about? You
wanna win doncha?'

I think, as I watch the argument tail off into mutual
disdain, the coven member grabbing her son's hand and

dragging him away towards their car, muttering and moaning as she goes, that I must have been blessed with the parents of my lads. What a great bunch they are: supportive, loyal, uncomplaining. They shout encouragement, they never undermine the team when it is losing; in Hamish's case they spend a lot of time going 'grrrrr' very loudly on the touchline. And none of them ever moans to me about how it would be better if I played their kid in a different position, or complains that someone else's son is playing while theirs is substitute, or issues contradictory instructions from the side.

Or at least that has been the case since Jeff left.

Doug told me, when I first started coaching the boys' team, that twelve was the difficult age.

'Twelve's the dangerous time,' he had said. 'Get past that intact and most likely you will stay together all the way through. But more teams split up at twelve than any other time. That's when the cliques start, see. That's when the bullying starts. That's when you have to watch it.'

It seemed a huge distance ahead back then, back when the boys were just eight. I couldn't believe little boys, so fresh and keen, big-eyed with enthusiasm, would ever grow into moaners or split into cliques. But still, I remembered what he had said; I remembered, too, what had happened to Hugo. And I said to Jeff at the start of the under-twelve season that we had to look out for it. If they started to get at each other, to issue mutual blame, then the whole team spirit would go. We had to foster an atmosphere of encouragement, otherwise the boys would take our lead and get on each others' back.

'Absolutely right,' he said. 'So we'd better watch them. Watch Gio, Tim, Rory. Them lot.'

'Those? Why?'

'JJ tells me they're devious.'

'But, Tim? Are you serious?'

'Get rid of them if they start. In fact, get rid of them now. It's the best way.'

'Well, I . . .'

'Up to you. Your funeral. But if you ask me, get rid.'

At under-twelve they had just started playing eleven-a-side matches on the big pitch. Suddenly, after the smaller pitches they had been used to, they looked out of scale, tiny. Now was the time that teamwork began to matter. You could no longer rely on one individual to win games for you, particularly not Lee who had moved to the local league club's academy. Now you needed all eleven players, plus the substitutes, just to work the ball up to the other end of the pitch.

Jeff was worried about JJ out there on the big pitch. He felt that the full-back position I had earmarked for the lad was not one in which he would flourish. He felt he needed a bigger platform.

'Move him forward to midfield, he could run the game from there,' he told me.

'Well, I've got Luke there on the left.'

'Well, move Luke back,' said Jeff. 'Or drop him. He's got a bad attitude anyway.'

Every week it was like this: Jeff's analysis of the team's performance was predicated on how JJ had played and whether I had played him in the right position.

'What did you think of Fraser today, I thought he did really well,' I'd say, trying to divert attention from the endless examination of JJ.

'Fraser? All right. Bad attitude though.'

Eventually, I succumbed to the nagging. Anything for

a quiet life, I gave JJ a go in midfield. Quite an extended go, at least four games. But he floundered. Unable to keep possession, he would routinely give the ball to an opponent. And every time he did so, he would turn to his father on the touchline and, keen to make sure everyone realised he was not responsible, offer a loud and detailed critique of his team-mates. As if living in constant terror that he might be blamed by the other players, he would get the blame in first:

'He wasn't running into space, Dad.' Or, 'Not my fault, he should have been there.' Or, 'He should have got that, he's crap.'

Satisfying himself that it was someone else's fault, he would never then try to recover from his own, let alone anyone else's mistakes. While Paul, Luke or Jamie were leather-lunged in midfield, tearing around trying to retrieve the ball when it was lost, JJ would give it away and then just stand there, arms held out, imploringly.

'JJ, track back,' I'd shout. And I could feel Jeff alongside me, hurting with every criticism.

Then I would try to substitute him. Most of the lads were brilliant when they were called off the pitch. They would copy what they had seen on the telly, and trot off clapping their hands above their head as if acknowledging a vast ovation, before exchanging high-fives with the boy coming on. Not JJ. He would sulk, he would drag his feet, he would look to his father with a desperate 'Dad?' He would start to cry: anything to stop me subbing him. And when he finally came off, he would routinely head straight for his father's car, demanding to be taken home, with Jeff following him, neither of them to return.

So I tried it the other way round, starting with him

on the touchline and bringing him on during the course of the game. But that, if anything, provoked even more desperation. He would stand by my side from the moment the game kicked off, buzzing round, pestering: 'When am I going on?'; 'Can I go on now?'; 'Take him off, he's useless.'

'Give it a few minutes, JJ mate,' I'd say. And he'd go and stand by his dad and start nadgering him. To his credit Jeff would never insist JJ came on, but I could sense his discomfort, sense his desperation that JJ go out there and prove to be the man.

Once Paul went down after a challenge in a manner that really worried me. Bundled off the ball, he was out flat and cold on the turf. Everyone round the pitch went quiet realising here was a serious problem. The opposition coach and I both ran on to the pitch to attend to him. As we leant over him, me pulling his tongue away from the back of his throat and laying him on his side, the referee taking out his mobile to put in a call for an ambulance, I felt a tug on my jumper. It was JJ.

'Can I come on now, then?' he said.

Boys are not stupid. Twelve-year-old boys in particular are sharper than a five-blade Gillette with battery-driven vibrating action. Alert to any nuance, alive to any sense of differentness, they home in on it with radar-like precision. You could see in the way they looked at each other when JJ made a fuss, or blamed them when he lost the ball, that there was something brewing, something beginning to fester. There was a boil growing there every time JJ told one of them that his dad was a better coach than Arsène Wenger or that his dad didn't like their attitude. And I didn't help things. Instead of taking Jeff to one

side and telling him I was worried about the way his
son was clearly not enjoying himself, I shrank from the
challenge. Trying to avoid confrontation, I would play JJ
more often than he deserved, single him out for praise
in the hope that encouragement would reap dividends,
excuse his tantrums. Every time I did it, I could see the
glances between the others. I should have done something, like Doug warned me I should. But I didn't. I let
it start to stew.

And twelve-year-old boys know what is going on. In
fact, they could give Machiavelli lessons in deviousness.
For work reasons, I was away a lot that season, and Jeff
took a number of training sessions. There was no faulting
his effort. He would spend hours preparing complicated
drills, sophisticated training-ground solutions to our many
faults. But they would never quite come off because the
boys weren't prepared to let them. They'd deliberately
make mistakes just to watch him descend into a comedy
fury. His sessions always ended in some sort of confrontation. He would be on the phone to me afterwards,
complaining about this boy, upset by that one. It wasn't
long before I started getting dads on the touchline after
matches, taking me by the elbow and saying, a hint of
anguish in their voices:

'Quiet word, just a bit worried about training with Jeff.
I don't know why, the lads don't seem to be enjoying it.'

That's the lads who were there, that is. Though he was
to come back later, Lee had left us the previous season.
And the likes of Patrice, Luke, Adam, Gio and Rory were
only a sporadic presence.

It was pretty clear what was happening: Jeff and JJ were
being what Barney would call 'rinsed', cold-shouldered,
isolated. Jeff's authority was being undermined by his

relationship with his son. Jeff was not a man to take such treatment in his stride, and he bristled at every turn. With every bristle, he was moving further from the boys. And me? I let it happen. My excuse to myself was that I needed someone to help, especially as I was away a lot midweek with work and Jeff was always there, always willing, always prepared to put in the time. Plus I fooled myself that there was nothing wrong with a good cop, bad cop approach to team bonding. After all, wasn't that what Brian Clough and Peter Taylor won two European Cups perfecting?

But the tension was ratcheting up to the point where sometimes you could hardly breathe. The loathing between JJ and the other boys was bubbling, boiling. One day, after JJ had missed not one, not two, but three open goals in a game, stabbing the ball tamely wide and then turning round and blaming Paul or Tim, or whoever it was for not passing it properly, I let my irritation spill to the surface.

As I made my way to the changing rooms after the game, JJ was alongside me, fizzing.

'Who was man of the match?' JJ was asking. 'Do you reckon I was? I reckon I was. My dad reckons I was. I thought I done really well today. Had loads of chances.'

And that's when all the frustration of biting my tongue and keeping quiet as he moaned and whinged and complained about being substituted came roaring upwards. Mind you, I was calm. And that is even more dangerous.

'JJ,' I replied, 'come with me a moment.'

I led him out on to the pitch and we walked together into the penalty area and stood either side of the penalty spot. Jeff was hovering, watching from a few yards off, alongside him a small crowd of boys and parents had gathered, watching too.

'JJ,' I said, loudly enough that everyone could hear, 'do you see that thing there?'

'Yes.'

'What is it?'

'It's a goal.'

'Yes that's right, JJ, well done,' I said, sarcastically. 'Now you know what it is, put the bloody ball in it next time.'

I then turned, walked to the car and drove off, Barney smiling to himself as he sat in the passenger seat.

Ten minutes after I got home, the phone rang, as I knew it would.

'You were way out of order there,' Jeff said. He was right, I was. It was a cruel, unnecessary thing to do to a twelve-year-old whose self-confidence made an eggshell look like tungsten.

'He's in pieces here,' Jeff continued. 'You know, it was so public what you said to him. They were all standing there watching, loving every minute of it. All of them, they've never liked us since we got here. Never made us welcome.'

'Look,' I said after a moment's silence had hung between us, 'I know it was me who asked you to come to the club, but maybe he'd be better off . . .'

'Oh no you don't,' he said. 'I know your game. It's as much our club as yours, so you can forget that. We're staying. You'd better sort it out. There's more than a few in there that you need to get rid of. And you need to be doing it quick.'

That was then. But today is now. And we have just earned ourselves a place in the cup semi-final. Which will be played at a proper ground, with stands, decent changing rooms and a fully functioning bar selling not just luke-warm tea, but beer and stuff. It was Rory who did it. He has proven himself to be the most fantastic of goalies since he took over from Max. His confidence, his agility, the security he brings, has completely altered the team. Suddenly we don't look as though we will be beaten. And today he makes save after save to keep us in the game.

Standing down the far end of the touchline, watching him dive and sprawl, catch and throw, is Max. He hasn't turned up at all since his disaster day, sending me the occasional apologetic email saying he has a cold or has strained a muscle. Today, though, he has appeared, ready to play as an outfield substitute. Unfortunately, he pulls something in the warm-up and starts to hobble.

'I'll only go on if it is an emergency', he says. But there isn't an emergency, not today when – with precious little input from the coach – everything sings like Charlotte Church and Shirley Bassey duetting at a Friday night karaoke in Tiger Bay. So he stays on the sidelines, occasionally clutching at his calf, or his ankle. And sometimes his other knee.

I can't help noticing him, standing there, trying to smile as all around him the parents and supporters cheer the guy who took over from him in goal. I can't help noticing his face, just after Rory makes yet another brilliant save, provoking Hamish to sustain a 'grrrrrrrrrr' for an eardrum-shattering ten seconds or more. There is the faint trace of a smile, but I can see it hurts. And later, just after I have been extravagantly high-fiving our new hero, I can sense him standing beside me, waiting to say something.

'Max, hey mate, how's the leg?' I say. 'Be all right for next week?'

'Maybe,' he says. And he pauses. 'I did tell you I wasn't a keeper, you know.'

He then walks away from the ground, his chin pointed into his chest, his mind clearly occupied with something other than cheery celebration.

19

Oh blimey

Malcolm has sent me an email demanding that Ian be stripped of all club membership and responsibility with immediate effect.

'This tea bar audit is clearly personally motivated, an attempt to undermine everything I am trying to build within the club,' he writes. 'The kettle is an essential part of an overall strategy for advancement of our situation. I'm sorry that you seem unable to see this, let alone back me publicly on the issue. I have attached an email outlining your support for my position and I would be grateful if you would circulate it as soon as possible. If you feel unable to do so, then at least I will know where I stand.'

I take a couple of Nurofen, seek out a darkened room and go and lie down.

20

The semi-final

Everything comes easy for the modern, middle-class British child. We live in the most affluent condition humankind has ever enjoyed. None of us go hungry; every material thing is available. Like many kids of their age, what the boys in my team want, they get. If Rory wants a mini-motorbike for his birthday, sure, he gets one. Arctic Monkeys CDs, iPods, new trainers: these are not an issue. When there is a school trip, Barney only has to ask if he can go and he does. Even at school when it comes to public exams, if the modern pupil buggers up a paper, they can retake it and retake it until they get a decent result. That is if the teacher or their mum hasn't done the coursework for them already.

That's what life in twenty-first-century Britain is like for a kid: if you want it, it will come. We live in a wishing-on-a-star world, a society of easy gratification in which the fruit machine always comes up on the jackpot.

There is just one place where wanting is not enough: sport. Out on the football field, or cricket pitch or athletic track, you can want as much as you like but desire alone will not deliver success. Every week I hear other coaches ask their players: 'Do you want this?' I've done it myself: 'Do you want this, boys?' And the answer is always a shouted, collective 'Yes.' But then they go and lose hopelessly, because this is the one part of their life where wanting is not enough. You have to work, you have to strive, you have to try. If you don't do those things, you don't get anything. If you don't put in the practice, your game deteriorates. If you don't put in the effort, you get no reward. But if you do, the rewards are tangible. For me, that is why sport is such a vital life lesson.

The opportunity my lads face this afternoon is one that will not come round often, if ever, again. It has to be seized now. And just wanting to win today and progress to the final is pointless. No one is going to buy a place for them (unless Rory's dad has come to some brown envelope arrangement with the referee without my knowledge). They will have to earn their passage there by working harder than any of them has ever worked before.

Or at least that is what I am telling Barney on the way to the cup semi-final. I'm rehearsing my pre-match speech, but Barn isn't listening. He has the car window open and is gulping in the fresh air.

'You OK?'

'Yep.'

'Sure?'

'Mmm.'

We had some people round last night and he'd acted as wine waiter, a fourteen-year-old sommelier. He seemed to think the job entailed sampling as much as pouring, a misconception greatly encouraged by my friends. From about eleven o'clock I'd tried to get him to go to bed, telling him he had a big game the next day. He had been about to go upstairs, when my mate Rob intervened.

'Don't listen to him, Barney,' he said. 'How old are you?'

'Fourteen.'

'Fourteen? You're supposed to ignore your father. That's what fourteen-year-olds do. Stay here with us.'

'I'm thinking of the football,' I said. Before adding, rather more pompously than I intended: 'I am his coach.'

'Yeah, yeah, next he'll be doing an Alex Ferguson and have you followed, Barney,' said Rob. 'Spies all over town. Keeping tabs on you. Ringing him up to tell him you're in a nightclub. Stay up, Barney, ignore him.'

Barney had grinned and chortled and carried on being the sommelier, much to everyone's good cheer. In the end, I think I went to bed before him.

So this morning he is not quite as fresh as he might be. I had left him to sleep until the last moment. When he got up, he spent ten minutes in the bathroom, the unmistakable sound of the morning after drifting down the stairs. His first hangover on the day of the biggest football game so far in his teenaged life.

'What the bloody hell kind of preparation is this?' I had said when he walked into the kitchen.

'Don't worry about it, Dad,' said his older brother, who was sitting at the table dressed only in a pair of boxer shorts, eating cereal. 'I thought that's what you said Sunday-morning football was supposed to be about, playing off the night before.'

'At my age maybe, but he's fourteen,' I'd said. 'Anyhow, what are you doing up? It's only midday.'

'I'm coming to the game,' he said. 'I am the Barmy Northmeadow Army. A one-man firm.

I've got an off pre-arranged with their mob.'

He is going to meet us there, he said, coming along later together with my wife and daughter. Oh yes, they've all emerged from the woodwork for this one. Rory alone is bringing about fifteen family members and Hamish rang me earlier this morning to ask if there were any seating facilities at the ground. He was bringing his aunt to watch Fraser play and she was a little frail.

'She's deaf as a post, too,' he said.

'Right,' I said. 'Well, make sure she sits next to you. She'll be the only person in the ground who can't be deafened by you.'

We arrive as we always do in a convoy of cars. Although half of the convoy take a wrong turn about two miles back, following Derek who has made a mistake keying the postcode into his sat-nav. We are playing at one of the non-league clubs locally, a proper ground, with a stand on one side, a low-rise shed covering the terracing at both ends, and a nightclub called 'Blazes' running down the length of one touchline. I note there are not one, but two fully operational tea bars in action. And the tea is hot. It is a big stage for fourteen-year-olds. They are even charging a pound at the gate entry fee. Though my older son's description of it as 'hallowed turf' turns out to be a little exaggerated: the pitch appears to consist solely of rolled mud, sogged up by a week of almost continual rain.

Unlike at our home ground, there are decent changing rooms here, though, with, on the wall, a whiteboard and a little plan of a football pitch marked on it. But we can't use the rooms because they are already filled with the clobber from the two teams who are in the middle of playing the other semi-final when we arrive. Barry has got there early and has watched them in action.

'Tell you what, they're not all that, either of them. I reckon we could do either of these when we get through to the final,' he says, his optimism unceasing.

Alongside him Lee, in jeans and sweatshirt, looks less cheery. He is, as he has been for most of the season, injured and will not take part in the game. The poor lad is a walking – well, hobbling – example of Brian McClair's assertion that you never can tell whether a kid will make it or not until they are at least fifteen. When he was nine there was no doubt in the mind of anyone who saw him that Lee was going to be a professional footballer. He was so much better than anyone else, he seemed to float through games as if propelled by some celestial force. Every week we would have scouts watching him. They would come from all over, and arrive trying to look anonymous, hoping to blend in with the parents, but forever giving the game away by sporting badges on their tracksuits boasting that they came from Chelsea, Reading, Southampton, Fulham or Coventry. He did have a year at a professional academy when he was eleven, but soon after he arrived he was injured, badly, and dropped out at the end of the year after only turning out for them about three times, his confidence as shattered as his carti-lage. Barry brought him back to us and for a while he was as great as ever. And the good news was, his dad came along too, to help once again with the coaching. But then the injuries started up once more. He was like a medical textbook. Tear, strain, rip, pull: he did the lot on an almost weekly basis. The problems would move up and down his legs, from groin to ankle, then occasionally break out and dislocate his shoulder or bruise his rib. This season he has played for us no more than four times. And the scouts have long ago taken their tracksuits elsewhere.

'He'll be back for the final, definitely,' says Barry, though Lee's smile is less confident.

'If we get there,' I say.

'When, mate, when,' he says. 'Everyone else here?'

'Everyone except Max. He emailed me to say he was injured. Said he might come to watch. Can't see him here, though.'

'So where's Barney?'

I nod along the touchline to where Barney is standing with both hands holding the crash barrier that runs round the edge of the pitch.

'Blimey, he's looking a little peaky. Is he OK?'

'Just nerves,' I say. 'He'll be fine.'

At which point Barney leans over the barrier and retches into the mud.

I have my pre-match speech prepared, but decide to ditch it as soon as I see the opposition arriving. They come from the toughest part of town, from the heart of the council estate that achieved national notoriety in the mid-nineties when the local youths would stage nightly dodgem races in cars pinched from the drives of the posh places to the north. Their team reflects the ethnic make-up of the new inner city. There are one or two Somalis in there, several children of Kosovan refugees, a couple of Albanians. And they are big and hard, pimp-rolling into the ground with their hoods up and their lips curled.

These are precisely the sort of opponents that Jeff used to reckon our lads would wilt against. He claimed that by the very nature of the social divide, estate kids would always win over the soft middle classes. And there is no denying most of my boys are middle class all right. They are the sons of accountants, teachers, salesmen, academics, even, in Fraser's case, the offspring of two artists. Only Lee can lay claim to a background similar to our opponents. And he is injured.

I gather the boys together in a huddle on the pitch, hurrying the latecomers who have finally found their way here despite Derek's machine. I remind them that the last time we played this lot, their big centre forward destroyed us single-footed. It was hard to miss him. Not only was he quick, strong, brave and at least a foot taller than most of our team, he sported an explosion of red hair that made him look as though his head was actually on fire. My daughter (who, despite insisting she is in fact strawberry-blonde, was once, when she was cycling to school, called a ginger slag by two workmen) tells me that ginge-ism is the last widely condoned prejudice and that it should be banned immediately. She has a point. From now on I dedicate myself to the new political battle: ginge-ism must stop. But not before I base my strategic briefing around this single idea: stop the ginge. I tell Tim to mark him; if we can keep him out of the game, we can match them everywhere else, I say. I had noticed, as he was warming up, that the ginge is wearing a bandage on his left knee.

'Push him on to his left foot, Timmy, all the time,' I say. 'Hit him hard in the tackle, Kal, boy. Let's see if he's just wearing that bandage for show.'

I finish by telling them not to be intimidated.

'Don't be scared of this lot,' I say. 'They're just a bunch of chavs who think they're hard. But really they are about as ghetto as Cliff Richard.'

As an analogy I might have chosen a more contemporary example: most of the players seem unsure as to who Cliff Richard is, never mind how ghetto he might or might not be. Tim looks at Gio and the two of them snort and giggle. And I don't think it is at the wit of my observation.

Barry and I watch the game from the technical area, a rectangle marked in whitewash in front of one of the dug-outs. It almost makes us feel like proper managers, particularly when the linesman asks me, after I have dashed down the touchline to shout something at Rory, to keep within it. Alongside us, in his technical area, is their coach, a chirpy scouser who directs an almost constant barrage of acid observations at the same linesman.

'Eh, lino, gorra problem with your shoulder? You hurtin', mate? Need a massage, la? No? Well, get yer arm in de air, den. He was so far offside he was in Birmingham, dat lad.'

It is not, in truth, a model game. It is scrappy, bitty, spoiled by a gusting wind that can't seem to make up its mind in which direction to blow. Neither side has a chance to score for the entire ninety minutes: the wide, wide pitch an obstacle too huge for rapidly wearying fourteen-year-old legs to overcome. Mind you, even the goalless, chanceless scrap going on here is a lot better to watch than the England match the day before, in which the self-styled gods of the sport appeared incapable of mastering the basics of the game, such as passing the ball to someone wearing the same-coloured shirt. Not that it should have come as a surprise. These days I increasingly find myself thinking the football I see lads play on a Sunday is more entertaining, more enterprising, more emotionally involving than the stuff served up by those playing in what likes to call itself the best league in the world.

It is certainly more honest. Despite the suggestion that kids will ape what they see in the professional game, I see no diving, no faking, no cheating here. There are tough tackles, though. And the surprising thing is, most of them are perpetrated by my lads. Of this I can be certain: these boys are not being intimidated. They are thudding into challenges, scared of no one. Some of the tackles – particularly on the ginge – would make me wince, if I wasn't secretly delighted by their aggression. And many of the more eye-watering are made by Barney, who has the game of his season. He gives, as he plunges through the mud in slide tackle after slide tackle, a bold refutation of the idea that the best preparation for football is an early night. There is not much more bolstering for the ageing ego than the vicarious thrill that runs through me when, after yet another tackle, half a dozen approving voices shout in unison round the ground: 'Well in, Barney.'

The boys are all magnificent today. But the one person who really makes the difference is Paul. He is a spiteful, snapping terrier in midfield, worrying the estate lads so much, they begin to back off as he approaches, giving him the room to dash and charge across the endless expanse of mud. I think, as he clatters into the increasingly lame ginge, bundling him off the ball and leaving him clutching at his knee, that you want a spiky kid in your team. You can understand why Alex Ferguson wanted Roy Keane and Eric Cantona at the heart of his efforts, why Rafa Benitez builds his team round Stevie Gerrard. You need someone on your side to make the opposition's life uncomfortable, who lifts his own side's morale by refusing to be cowed. And Paul is doing that and more. Mind you, Jeff might have been right about one thing: it could be in the genes. After all Paul, the nastiest, most aggressive, most driven player on the pitch by some measure, is the son of a lawyer.

Throughout the first half, in the shed behind one of the goals, Hugo has been shouting out encouragement, an unstoppable noise machine, his output matched only by the Hamish growl echoing out of the main stand. At half-time, I notice the two of them get together and for the second half they keep up an almost continual barrage of chanting, drawing around them a small choir which consists largely of Rory's relatives. If the lads are enjoying it half as much on the pitch as Hugo, Hamish and their acolytes are in the stands, then they are having the time of their life.

The game is eventually won in extra time by a penalty. And – peg out the bunting, ring the church bells and shout so loudly they can hear you in Wolverhampton – it is won by us. Kal scores it after Paul has been upended in the area charging goalwards. I try to stay calm, stay mature, stay dignified, especially as their manager is standing only a few yards away, his head down in disappointment. But I can't. And my celebrations include kissing a rather alarmed Barry on the cheek.

The ideas nicked from McClair and the others have begun to pay off. Simple training involving lots of ball work, small-sided games in which habits of passing and moving can be acquired and then applied to the bigger game, have made a huge difference to confidence and performance. Maybe it is not rocket science after all.

The feeling after it is over is a joy. The parents form a guard of honour and clap the shattered and battered lads off the pitch, their pride lighting up a grey afternoon. Each and every one of them comes up to Barry and me afterwards and thanks us.

'Eh, don't thank us, thank your boy,' says Bazz. 'He's the one who did it. Not us.'

And he is right. What the boys have done is work themselves to the point of exhaustion to achieve something. They wanted it, all right. But they worked for it, too. All Barry and I did was stand in our technical area shouting.

After a celebratory drink in Blazes, after slapping everyone I can find on the back, after buying Hugo and Hamish a whisky each to soothe their throats, I eventually find Barney in the dressing room, alone, sitting slumped on the bench, his head between his knees, mud smeared all over his legs, his hands, his face. He is utterly knackered.

'Brilliant, son,' I say. 'Proud of you.'

He looks up and manages an exhausted smile.

'Dad,' he says. 'I'm dead. Why didn't you send me to bed early last night?'

Looking back on it, as I do quite often over the next few days, what strikes me most about the afternoon is the attitude of the opposition. Barney tells me on the way home how he had played rugby at an expensive boarding school the week before and the home team had constantly given it mouth, thinking they were hard and street and then tried to pick a fight after losing, even chucking all their visitors' clothes into the dressing-room showers and soaking them in revenge for defeat.

'Seriously, Dad, you should have heard them,' he says. 'They really did think they were a bunch of Gs. It was pathetic.'

And yet here were the lads from the roughest part of town, who were genuinely hard, but according to Barney, never once did they mouth off or try to intimidate. I felt ashamed that I had been so dismissive of them in my pre-match chat. These kids were hugely impressive in defeat,

shaking hands, congratulating our lads. There was no petu-
lance, no sulking. The ginge was particularly gracious after
the game, wishing me good luck in the final.

'Win it for us, eh, mate,' he said.

They behaved, these guys, like gentlemen. I don't know
if there is a life lesson here, but this game just continues
to confound every known stereotype.

As for me, my state of high excitement lasts for a couple
of days after the victory. I spend far too much time when
I should be working checking the boys' league website,
reading the postings about it on the message board, like the
one from someone calling himself a long-time observer of
boys' football, saying that the game restored his faith in sports-
manship. Then, to top it all, I get a call from the manager
of the county representative side. He was at the game on
Sunday, he says, and would like to invite some of our players
along for trials. At last they have been recognised.

My thrill, however, is short-lived. A couple of days after
the big game, I am on my way to the office when I get
a call on my mobile.

'Is this Mr White?' asks a voice.

'Yes.'

'The chair of Northmeadow Youth Football Club?'

'Yes.'

'It's Des Lewis from the council here, Mr White. I
wonder if you could come down to the playing fields
immediately.'

'Why?'

'There has been a break-in at the clubhouse. We need
you to come down to verify what – if anything – has
been stolen.'

Oh God, somebody has turned over the tea bar. I
wonder if they nicked Malcolm's kettle?

21

It's a jungle in here

'My God,' says the man from the council as he steps over the upturned chairs, the pile of sweaty shirts, the goal nets lying strewn across the floor, 'they've turned this place over a treat.'

'Actually,' I say, picking up a training bib that has long ago been dampened to use as a dishcloth and is now covered in a sheen of grey mould, 'it's pretty much always like this.'

We are in the tea bar, following the break-in. Someone has levered off the padlock on the outside door and booted through the inner door. Burglars in search, presumably, of money. Maybe they thought there was a vending machine in here. Or perhaps a petty cash tin. I can only assume they were looking for something a little more substantial than a wholesale packet of coffee creamer and a past-its-sell-by-date box of Wagon Wheels.

'So what has been stolen?' the council man asks.

'To be honest, I've no idea,' I say. 'Thing is, I'm not sure what was here in the first place.'

'I see,' he says, turning a couple of pages over on the

clipboard he is carrying. 'You have no idea. And yet you say you are the chairman of the club?'

Yeah, I think, that does about sum it all up.

As we make our way out of the tea bar, towards the trophy room, we have to step over the inner door, which is lying where it fell. It wobbles slightly as I put my foot on it. It is propped up against something. Between us, the bloke from the council and I, we lift the door up and put it back on its hinges. And there on the floor, lying smashed and almost flattened by the force of the intrusion, is a catering-sized kettle. Malcolm's thirty-five-quid catering-sized kettle.

22

The scene of the crime

We are in the cup final, yet are still in danger of relegation. Which makes us the Brighton-in-1983 of boys'
football. Or maybe the Middlesbrough-in-1997. I had
hoped that the momentum from the semi win would
carry us through to league safety. But the trouble with
momentum is that it takes no account of how other teams
fare. I wrote on a sheet of paper a projection of what
might happen in the season's remaining fixtures. I gave a
possible points total for us and each of our four rivals for
the second relegation spot (the bottom team are already
as good as down). My extrapolations conclude that we
would avoid the drop by a clear five points. Every week,
I have compared real scores to those on my sheet. So far,
thanks to a couple of Kal-inspired wins and a brilliant
draw with the league leaders, my projection of our final
points total is uncannily on track. Unfortunately I had
cheerily assumed all the other teams would be losing left,
right and centre. One of them, I had down as not getting
another point. In the month since I committed my predic-
tions to paper they have won every game. After every

Sunday, after each round of fixtures, I scan the league tables on the website and see we are still not safe.

'We must be,' says Barney.

'We're not,' I say. 'Check this out.'

Barney and I discuss it endlessly. Do I think we'll make it? he'll ask over breakfast. What formation does he think we should use? I'll ask him when he comes home from school. Is Lee going to be fit? he'll ask after supper. Where recently there was silence, now there is speculation; where there was division, now there is obsession; where there was distance, now there is the league table. Well, it fills a hole.

Besides, it is almost like therapy to be able to share this madness, albeit with a fourteen-year-old kid. Though the two of us sitting in front of the computer checking the website every five minutes is starting to raise the hackles of other members of the household.

'Like the rest of the world gives a damn,' my daughter will say when she catches us at it. 'Why don't you ask me about my life for a change?'

'Sorry, you're right,' I'll say. 'What would you like me to ask you?'

'Well, for a start you could ask me if I've got a Glastonbury ticket yet.'

'OK, Els: have you got a Glastonbury ticket yet?'

'No,' she'll say. There will then be a pause.

'So that was a long conversation,' I'll say.

'Yeah and whose fault's that?' she'll snap back and then she'll storm dramatically, ostentatiously, with a theatrical flick of her fringe, out of the room.

'Watch the door,' I'll say as she slams it.

'Watch your face,' she'll shout back.

'Right,' I'll say to Barney as she leaves. 'Where were

we? If St Joseph's beat Hough End, where does that leave Littlebourne?'

Today we are playing another side in the lower reaches of the league. John Motson would characterise it as a relegation six-pointer. A win here will just about save us. I have to leave at half-time, sadly. I'm covering a match in Manchester, a Premiership title-decider. It shows how my passion has shifted that when the paper asked me, I was reluctant to accept the assignment. Once I'd have lobbied and chivvied and bullied for weeks to get the job; these days, if I had the choice I'd rather sidestep free admission to the game everyone in the country is talking about, the one for which touts will be charging a hundred and fifty quid a ticket outside the ground, the one that has filled the back pages of the newspaper with gossip and speculation for the past three weeks, so that I can watch a bunch of fourteen-year-olds labour about a council pitch. At one point, I even consider feigning sickness to get out of it. But I pull myself together, tell myself to grow up. It is what I am paid to do, after all.

Still, a Sky-friendly late kick-off means I can drive some of the lads over to their morning game on my way north and catch the first half. In the back of the car is Max. He hasn't been around much recently, didn't even come to watch the semi-final, but he is here today, happy to start as sub, he tells me, ready to come on if necessary on the left side of midfield, he says. That's fine by me, I tell him. And I just hope that today he can enjoy himself, relaxed and free of the pressure. Not that he looks relaxed. Barney tries to engage him in conversation, but he doesn't say much in the car. Instead, it's left to Barney and me to speculate, endlessly, about the day's other games and how they will affect the league standings.

We turn up at the appointed venue only to discover the rival manager waiting with news. There has been a booking mix-up, another team is using their pitch and we are to play instead at the big council playing field complex down the road. So we set off in convoy following his directions, Derek slipping in behind me, no longer content to trust his sat-nav. As I drive near, I begin to get an uncomfortable feeling, a sticky sense of déjà vu. It is confirmed as I swing into the car park. This is it. We may have come by a roundabout route, but there is no doubt about it: I recognise the pub on the corner, the children's playground with its mound and zip wire, the changing rooms that still have the same graffiti on the outside wall suggesting that our home town is full of batty boys. Barney recognises it, too.

'Hey, isn't this the place?' he says as he gets out of the car.

It is the place all right. This is where that fateful tournament was held two long, long years ago. This is where it all finally happened with Jeff.

There aren't quite so many people here today as there were back then, on that hot May afternoon when it seemed most of the population of the county had gathered to witness it all kick off, to stand round and tut, to shake their heads and wonder what the world was coming to. It was a big event that was being staged on the ground that day, the biggest junior tournament for miles around. There were marquees and gazebos, barbecues and refreshment stalls. It looked like the tented village at Wimbledon. Though without the two-quid-a-mouthful strawberries.

Hundreds of parents turn up at tournaments like this with their offspring, to eat awful burgers, to buy long, sticky shoelace sweets and most of all, to park their cars. Now these could just be left across the road from where the tournament is being held, but the club hosting the event makes money from charging them to park on one of their fields. And, despite the fact that they have been to tournaments before and know that they will be charged for parking, despite the fact that this is really just a way of delivering a charitable donation to keep boys' football afloat, there will be at least three drivers in every ten who affect surprise at having to pay to park.

'Three quid?' they will say. 'Bloody hell, you need a mortgage to park round here.'

We arrived at the ground behind an enormous SUV, equipped with burnished steel bull bars just in case the driver were to encounter an enraged Aberdeen Angus on the way to Waitrose. It was sitting so high above the road you needed a set of stepladders to climb up to the driver's door. It growled to a stop and the window slid down and the boy collecting money at the gate reached up on tiptoes to inform the driver of the cost. Clearly the entrance fee was a point of contention. After a brief altercation with the boy, the vehicle's reversing lights suddenly came on and the muscular beast moved rapidly in the direction from which it had come. When it drew level with my car, the tinted front window came down with a quiet hum and, leaning across the passenger seat, looking down on my battered, tattered old machine was a one-time Premiership footballer, a celebrity hereabouts.

'Can you just move forward so I can back out?' he said.

'You not going in?' I said.

'You're joking. I ain't paying three quid to park in a field. I'm here to present the trophies and they're trying to make me pay up. They must think I'm made of bleedin' money.'

So that's how he affords to live in that gated mansion in the poshest end of town, I thought as I steered my car into the hedge to allow him to pass. Look after the pennies and the Baby Bentleys will look after themselves. After I had paid my money and parked up, we walked through a mini-fairground of attractions. There were penalty shoot-outs, a tombola, plus a raffle with a first prize of the chance to meet a certain recently retired celebrity footballer once he had parked his motor. There was a bouncy castle, too, which was later to be overrun by feral eight-year-olds brushing aside the volunteer in charge and attempting to free it from its moorings. Next to it was a sign saying the advertised hot air balloon rides had had to be withdrawn. Apparently, the day before, half the team in the final of the under-nines competition had ended up at kick-off time marooned some-where over Milton Keynes after the balloon caught a thermal.

Like at most junior football tournaments round our way, the fringes of the playing fields had bloomed into a showcase of canvas. All round were tents in which parents were lounging in deckchairs, their feet on cool boxes, beer in hand, kitted up for the long haul. Some had brought umbrellas and sun shades, others fold-up picnic tables and disposable barbecues.

Where our team had established itself, however, it was not quite so decorous. For some reason we have never quite mastered sufficiently high levels of construction skills to become the sort of operation that sets up camp at tour-naments. Early in our existence we did take a gazebo along to one. But even with Barry's building-site expertise marshalling us, it took six of us nearly half an hour to erect it, a small crowd gathering to applaud our cack-handed progress. And then, while we were pegging out the last of the guy ropes, one of the boys, after a visit to the barbecue, had slipped into it and thrown up, depositing a slick of half-digested burger down one of the inside walls. No one fancied using it thereafter. Even when it started to rain, we all stood around outside, while the puddle of sick stayed nice and dry inside.

So that day you could spot our encampment from a mile off by its lack of facilities. It was just a few bits of discarded clothing, some plastic bags and a couple of footballs (though not for long, Gio had soon ballooned one of them into the scrubland behind the playing fields, where it was swallowed up by an area so ill-kempt and overgrown there was probably a Japanese soldier living in there, convinced the war was yet to end). But, despite the dearth of tented accommodation, the results that day were good. Lee had completed his injury-plagued season with the academy and Barry had rung me to ask if he could turn out for us. I was thrilled, and, largely thanks to his unerring eye for goal, we had progressed through the group stages with a flourish.

Jeff wasn't due to arrive until later in the afternoon, which may have been one reason why things were so relaxed on and off the pitch. JJ was there, but, without his dad in attendance, he was unusually quiet, not his nadgering self at all. It had only been a couple of weeks since the 'that's the net' incident, so I assumed he was still wary of me. As Lee destroyed team after team, JJ seemed content to stand on the touchline as a non-participating member of the squad, occasionally telling the opposition supporters and substitutes that that was his best mate out there, scoring all those goals and that all the clubs in the Premiership were after him.

When we got to the semi-final, I said to JJ:

'Don't you fancy a run out?'

'I'm all right.'

'Come on, JJ. You don't want to miss out on this, it's the semi-final.'

'Nah, don't want to.'

So we started without him, and were soon two goals up; Lee shredding their defence on each occasion. Then, with only a couple of minutes to go, suddenly JJ was on my shoulder:

'I wanna come on, I wanna come on, let me on,' he said.

'I thought you didn't want to play.'

'Do now,' he said. 'C'mon, it's not fair if you don't.'

I called Barney over to be substituted. There were rolled eyes as JJ trotted on in his ungainly fashion, a look passed between Lee and Gio. Rory was less discreet.

'What's he coming on for?' he called out to Tim. 'Why's he taking Barney off for him?'

I couldn't work out JJ's change in attitude until I heard the shout from behind me: 'Give it JJ.' It was Jeff. JJ must have seen him parking his car in the road that abutted the pitch and was suddenly animated, anxious to get out there.

'Ah, Jeff,' I said.

'How's it going?' Jeff said.

Before I could answer, he was shouting at Lee, who had possession:

'Give it JJ. He's in acres . . .'

Lee didn't and lost the ball, shooting Jeff a thin-eyed glance as he did so.

'Bloody hell, I thought he'd spent the season at the academy. So when's he going to learn to pass a football?'

I tried to tell him that it was only because of Lee that we were now in the final, but he was off away down the touchline, shouting at JJ:

'Work him, work him, go on son.'

The whistle had soon gone and I had duties out on the pitch, shaking hands with the opposition manager and ruffling the hair of our triumphant players.

'We done it,' JJ said to his father as the pair met in the centre circle.

'Get in there,' said Jeff. I just hoped he hadn't heard Gio's stage whisper, as he walked past: 'What do you mean, you did it?'

The final was not for an hour, because there were two other age-group finals to be played before it. I gave Kal a tenner and told him to go off and buy the lads ice creams. Jeff was not best pleased with the news of the delay.

'I've only just got here, now I've got to hang around for an hour. Sod it, I've got to go and finish some shopping. I'll be back for the final.'

JJ was beside him.

'Can I come, Dad?'

'No, stay here, boy. Anyway, I might not be back in time for the kick-off. You don't want to miss that, do you?'

JJ looked imploringly. But there was no changing his mind. And as his dad disappeared towards the car park, JJ trudged a few yards behind the other boys in the direction of the ice-cream stall.

I was sitting on a park bench with Barry and Gio's mum, drinking surprisingly hot tea bought from the tea bar, when Tim came running over.

'It's all kicked off between JJ and Rory.'

'What's happened?'

'I dunno, but you'd better come.'

In the middle of the children's playground behind the refreshment stalls, there was a mound, a man-made little hillock, from which led a zip-wire ride. Lots of kids in football kit were gathered round the bottom of the mound, not saying anything, just staring up at what was going on at its top, licking their ice creams and watching the show. Up there was JJ. He was standing on the summit, swinging a metal pole above his head. Circling him were Lee, Gio and Rory.

'What the hell is going on?' I shouted, at which Lee, Gio and Rory quickly tried to disappear off into the crowd.

'Oi, oi, not so fast, you lot,' I said. 'What's going on here?'

'He started it,' the three of them chorused.

'Right, bugger off back to the base camp and wait for me there, I'll calm him down.'

I told JJ to put the pole down and get off the mound. He was raging, smashing the pole into the ground and shouting how he was going to kill them and how he hated them and how he wanted to bash their heads in. The kids standing round the mound had now been joined by a few parents, who stood there, enjoying the spectacle.

'Come on, JJ, come down,' I said. Maybe he caught sight of the gathering crowd, maybe he had a change of heart, maybe he just got bored, but he chucked the pole into some scrub and came down. We went off for a walk together. It was a sad trudge. Misery was apparent in every step. He was distraught, gabbling his complaints, hurt and fury spilling out in equal measure. If ever there was a time a kid needed an arm round the shoulder it was this. But I hesitated, remembering the bloke at the dinner party and his assumptions about the motives of those who coach children. Worried how it might look, I offered him no comfort.

'I hate them, I hate them,' he was saying. 'I never want to play for this team again.'

'JJ, son, son, what's all this about?' I said.

'They told me I was useless and I only got on the team because my dad was the coach and I told them they'd never have got anywhere with their stupid team if my dad hadn't done everything.'

'Hey, JJ, for a start you're not useless . . .' I said. But he wasn't listening.

'They said I was thick and useless. I just want to go home. Where's my dad?'

By now I was pretty pissed off. Sure, JJ could be a pain in the neck, but this was bullying, pure and simple. This was what happened to my own son all those years ago. I patched him up and persuaded him to come back to the base camp, where I told Tim to take him off for an ice cream.

'I don't want to go with him, I hate him,' said JJ. Tim looked perplexed, so I signalled to Barney and Kal to take JJ off. They did, but without any real conviction. While they were gone I confronted the others.

'What's going on?' I said to Rory.

'Why you getting at me? Why are you blaming me? You always blame me, you and him.'

'Rory, I'm only asking what was going on.'

'He started it. Look at my shirt,' said Rory, pointing to a jagged tear running down the front of his football kit. 'He just attacked me with that metal, said he was going to nail me. I hate him.'

'He said you were calling him names, saying he was useless and only was in the team because his dad's the coach.'

'Well, it's true,' said Rory. 'Anyway, he started it saying we were useless and his dad had said we were never going to win anything with us lot in the team. He said his dad was going to make sure we didn't play any more. I think his dad's a dickhead.'

We really were in trouble here. Deep, deep trouble.

'Listen, boys,' I said. 'Let's just shake hands with him and be nice to him and see if that makes a difference.'

'Get lost, I'm not touching his hand. Or his dad's hand. You don't know where it's been.'

Luke started sniggering at that. A couple of others joined in. I could see Luke mime the process of shaking someone's hand then looking at it and wiping it on his shorts.

'Look, just shake hands, OK?'

It took some persuasion, but eventually they agreed to call a truce, though hands remained resolutely unshaken. Meanwhile, word had got out among the parents what had happened. Rory's dad came up to me and said:

'What's he done?'

'Don't worry about it, I think it's sorted. He's been arguing with JJ, basically.'

'God, he's irritating.'

'Who, JJ or Rory?'

He just grinned at that one.

By now there were only a few minutes until the final. The game before was coming to an end, so, once the ice-cream party had returned with a now much calmer-looking JJ, I took the boys over to the pitch where a younger age group were playing, sat them down behind one of the goals and told them . . . well, yes, I told them to shut their eyes and imagine that trophy, imagine what they might do to make sure they got their hands on it, imagine scoring the winning goal. That trophy was theirs, I said, so just think how they'd feel if someone else went home with it. Perhaps it was the calm after the row, perhaps it was the proximity of winning something at last, whatever the reason, they all sat there with their legs crossed and eyes shut, quietly, thoughtfully. There was no giggling, no smart-arsing, no joshing. Even Luke was giving a reasonable impression of sitting there in deep concentration.

'My God,' I thought. 'They've bought into this. It might work.'

'OK,' I said. 'Now imagine scoring that winning—'

I didn't see him until he was almost in the middle of the group. It was Jeff, roaring, raging. He had come back from his shopping trip and had met Barry at the tea bar. Bazz had told him that there'd been a bit of a problem between JJ and one of the other lads, but it was now all sorted. But Jeff wasn't listening. He was going to fight his son's battle. He had come straight over to where they were sitting in a circle, and headed for Rory.

'I bet it was you, wasn't it?' he was saying. 'It's always bloody you, you spoiled little . . . You lay off my son, right.'

Rory was so taken aback by the force of the incursion, for perhaps the first time in his life he was lost for words. I grabbed Jeff by the arm.

'Jeff, mate, come on,' I said.

'Me come on? Me? I turn my back for half an hour and the whole thing kicks off. It's a shambles. My son's been attacked.'

'Jeff, Jeff, please, it's over, we've got a final in five minutes . . .'

The boys were still in their circle, most still sitting

cross-legged. But now, instead of eyes shut, they were round-eyed, staring up at us, astonished. By now, Rory's dad had arrived on the scene. He grabbed at Jeff's shoulder in an attempt to pull him back. I tried to manoeuvre myself between the two of them. Jeff struggled to free himself of Rory's dad's grasp. The force of his escape bid toppled him into me. I felt myself tumbling over backwards and, reaching out for support, grabbed at their shirts. As I fell, I merely succeeded in pulling the pair of them down on top of me. We landed, the three of us, on the back of the goal.

As we did so, on the pitch, the game in progress came shuddering to a halt. All the players stopped and stared. The parents flanking the touchline stood in gape-mouthed astonishment as the three of us struggled in the netting, pushing, shoving, trying to right ourselves. The first person to react was the referee who dashed round the back of the goal to where we were grappling and stood over us, blowing loudly three times on his whistle. As I lay there sprawled on the net, I looked up at the source of the whistle. I looked up his legs, past his knees, to his shorts. I could recognise the crease in those shorts anywhere. It was the pedant.

'And what exactly do you think you are doing?' he said. 'Do you think you might conduct business elsewhere while these eight-year-old boys conclude their football match?'

We lost the final that day. Let's just say the concentration was broken. After the game, Rory's dad told me he would be taking his son away from the club if Jeff remained.

'The man's a liability,' he said.

He was not alone in his concerns. Gio's mum said Jeff

was awful when I wasn't around, shouting at the kids and swearing. Hamish said Fraser had never liked him. Paul's dad said he was going to mention something ages ago, but didn't like to because Jeff was my old mate. But I just thought, Hang on a minute, Jeff was a bloke doing his best, who had given a lot of his time for nothing. Besides, who was being bullied here? And wasn't I as much to blame? I had seen it coming and done nothing about it.

Jeff and JJ had stormed off straight after the altercation, not staying for the final. I had a long, unhappy email from Jeff on my computer when I got home, all about how he was disappointed by my attitude, sorry that I hadn't seen what was going on and taken his side, especially as we had known each other for so long. At the end of it, though, he apologised and said he was embarrassed by his lack of control and that it would never happen again. Next season, he wrote, we would win the league, definitely. The team will really be going places once we'd got rid of all the troublemakers.

And I thought, This is it, isn't it? It's him or them. Jeff or half the team. I remembered my older son's experience. Remembered how he had suffered from the bullies. Remembered how disappointed I had been that his coach had preferred to remain oblivious to it, let it happen. And here I was doing exactly the same.

I rang Doug for advice. Both Jeff and Rory's dad had already been on to him before me, each demanding that the other be removed from the club.

'Who's at fault here?' Doug said.

I told him it was complicated, that Jeff's son was certainly being bullied but that his very presence was causing unhappiness, not least for the lad himself.

'OK, well, what do you think should be done?'

'I dunno, that's why I'm ringing you.'

'Well,' he said. 'You have to do what you feel is best and right for your team. But you have to do it now. This can't drag on.'

The choice was stark. Either back Jeff, which morally in this circumstance might well be the right thing to do, but which would, inevitably and certainly, lead to the destruction of the team. At least five of the boys would not turn out for us again, and most of the other parents would not allow their child to carry on with him in a position of authority. Or ask him to take JJ somewhere else. There could be no compromise.

Before I decided what to do, I asked someone who really mattered what he thought. Someone who had seen it all, observed it with an increasingly bemused eye. Someone who was there in the middle of it all. I gave Barney the two options and his reply sealed it.

'That's not really a choice, is it?' he said.

It was the most painful conversation I have ever had.

'Hi, Jeff, it's me. I've been thinking about what happened yesterday,' I began.

'Right,' he interrupted me. 'So, what are you going to do about it, then?'

I explained that I felt that JJ had been unhappy for some time and that his happiness must come first and it might be best for him to go to another club, where he could make a fresh start, away from an environment which had become too fraught for him.

'I see,' he said. 'So basically you're going to sack me because my son was being bullied. Well, you've shown your true colours.'

'Jeff, it's nothing to do with you.' Which was a lie for a start.

'I'm thinking of JJ,' I said. 'How can he stay on when he is in a state of war with every single player in the team? I mean, he's even fallen out with Tim.'

'You're not thinking of JJ. If you were thinking of him you'd get rid of the other lot. You're thinking of yourself. Don't pretend you're doing this for anyone else but yourself. Don't try and kid me this has been about anyone but you from the start.'

So it went on, for nearly two hours. He was right in most of what he said about me and how I had responded to the problem, though he was wrong in every detail about the boys: they were the best bunch of lads you could imagine, not the half-crazed Lord of the Flies psychos he maintained. At the end of the conversation, when he put the phone down on me after saying that a man can be judged not by his words, but by his actions and that my actions were indefensible, I knew it was over. As I put down the phone, it felt as if the clouds had suddenly parted. And that the sun was beaming down on my face.

'What you smiling about?' my wife said when I eventually came back downstairs.

'I'm free,' I said. 'Free at last, free at last.'

And I pulled her towards me and together we waltzed round the kitchen.

It doesn't mean it has been straightforward since. Or easy. At this place in particular, we don't have much luck. Maybe someone in Rory's past was the local landowner and dispossessed a bunch of gypsies who put a curse on him, a curse so long-lasting it lives on to nause up the lives of future generations. Maybe Jeff applied a hex on it as he stormed off that May afternoon. Maybe I'm just doomed.

When I leave for Manchester, though we have missed a good half-dozen chances to close it, we are 1-0 up and in complete control of the game. So dispirited were the opposition, their linesman – one of their parents – subjected them to a foul-mouthed tirade throughout. I happened to be standing by him when their centre forward, clean through on goal, shot and Barney hero-ically cleared.

'Fuck me, he's fucking useless,' he said, so loudly the kid must have heard.

'Well, you have to say he was unlucky. It was a magnif-icent clearance.'

'That? Nah. Donkey could have done that. Anyone could have cleared a shit shot like that.'

As I drive off, I think: That's it, we're safe. They will be five points behind us now, sitting in the second rele-gation spot. They'll never catch us.

Barry calls me when I am just south of Birmingham.

'You're not going to believe this,' he says.

'Go on,' I say.

'We were 2-0 up with ten minutes to go . . .'

'And?' Somehow, by his tone, I can tell there is an and.

'And . . . we lost. 3-2.'

There's a silence.

'Hello?' he says.

'Bazz, how did that happen?' I say.

'Thing was, Rory got injured and had to come off. So I asked Max if he'd come on in goal. He said he didn't mind . . .'

I get the full story from Barney later. Much later. When I first ring home to speak to him, his mother tells me he is in such a bad mood he has put himself to bed. We speak on my way back down from Manchester.

It seems Max came on for Rory and within a few moments had made two absolute howlers, let in the softest of goals, the first when he air-kicked at a back pass. But even a draw would have been a result for us. Then, with only seconds left of the game, the opposition had won a free-kick on the edge of the area. Our defence had sprung the offside trap, but the linesman, one of our parents, had not flagged. Everyone stood and looked at him apart from one of their kids, who just tapped the ball past Max. Apparently, the referee had even gone over to the linesman after the goal and said, are you sure they're not offside, because there's only ten seconds to go and if I give this goal, that's it, you've lost. And the linesman had said he could have cheated, but in his opinion they weren't offside when the kick was taken. Barney is still, eight hours after the event, fuming.

'Why couldn't he have cheated?' he says. 'Every other team's linesmen cheat. Everyone cheats. All he had to do was put that flag up. It's not like anyone would have minded. They all thought they were offside anyhow.'

'Well,' I say, trying not to reveal quite how seething I felt myself. 'You don't want to win by cheating. I mean, really you should never have been in that position that it mattered.'

'It's just so unfair. And I tell you what if we do go down, Max's going to get slapped.'

'Hey, it's not just his fault. It's a team game, everyone has to share the responsibility.'

'Dad, you weren't there. I'm telling you, he'll get slapped.'

Poor Max. After the game, distraught at his own culpability, he is too embarrassed to ask any of the parents to give him a lift home. Barry, who has to stay behind to fill in the match paperwork, spots him at a bus stop about half an hour later. He picks him up. Max sits in the back of the car with Lee and Gio. There is silence, Barry tells me. A long, long silence all the way home.

23

Europe

Still, at least we have qualified for Europe. As it happens, we qualified anyway. It is our turn. Every year during the Easter holidays a couple of age groups from the club go across to Holland, accompanied by managers, parents and most of Doug's extended family. This year we are the ones in line to head over for an international tournament held in a small Dutch town memorable for not much more than the fact it is near the Belgian border. The club has been undertaking trips like this since the days when Marco van Basten and Ruud Gullit were smoothly slicing open the English defence in the European Championships. In all that time, the trophy has returned to England only once. Most years managers come back with tales of humiliation at the feet of Dutch wunderkinds, with their total football and their Cruyff turns, annulling our attacks, making mockery of our midfield, doing our defenders. And the Germans aren't bad either. Our traditional role in the competition is to be game losers, a banker international victory, the equivalent of Luxembourg and San Marino in World Cup qualifiers. Or England in the finals.

No wonder they welcome us with open arms. Here come the patsies.

But never mind the results, it is the stories the boys' fathers tell each other afterwards of the hospitality, of the camaraderie, of the wacky baccy cafes that keep us going back. Losing every match is but small beer; it is the large amount of beer drunk in the Dutch clubhouse bar (no lukewarm tea here) that counts. We are cheered not by adding silverware to the trophy cupboard, but by tales of the year the under-twelves' manager lost his trousers after an all-night drinking session, the year three of the lads lost themselves somewhere in town following a Saturday night out that turned inevitably into Sunday morning, not to mention the year someone lost his dignity with a blow-up doll bought in the local sex shop. The doll eventually found its way back home and wafted around the tea bar for a month or so, until an angry mother applied a pin to its inflated upholstery after finding a couple of the under-eights playing keepy-uppy with it.

'Mum,' they had asked, 'why's her mouth open?'

We meet at five in the morning outside the tea bar. Doug, although no longer chairman, although no longer officially involved in the organisation, although his sons have now all graduated through the club away to adult football, is still in charge of the Dutch tour. He always has been and we can only assume he always will be. He loves it, he tells me as he stands there checking numbers, making sure everyone's remembered their passport, directing people into buses, his hacking cough loud enough to wake the neighbourhood. The Dutch, he wheezes, are his kind of people. And he is prepared to put up with the gripes, the late payments, the puddles of vomit deposited on the floor of the coach by travel-sick under-twelves who have already consumed their packed lunch before we have hit the motorway, in order to go over and see them.

'Yeah but, Doug,' I say to him, 'you could just go on your own. You don't have to take us with you, you know.'

'Nah,' he says. 'Wouldn't be the same without you lot getting in the way, would it?'

He has an entourage trailing in his wash, including his three sons, his wife and a nephew, plus his next-door neighbours, a couple called Steve and Andrea, who come on the tour every year, even though they have no children of their own. Doug has booked two coaches on the cheap ('Cash, saves on VAT'), vehicles of such vintage their last run-out may well have been to bring back home the participants on the Aldermaston marches. Mike's under-twelves climb into one coach. Giggling and chatty, bright-eyed and excited, my boys push and shove each other into the coach, where they take possession of the back seats. They are all here, except Max. He has not been around since his last and what has proven to be final debacle in goal. I have tried to contact him by email and on his mobile. But he is not answering. It is clear he has no wish to speak to me. And no wonder: I am the root of his humiliation. I asked Tim at training the other night if he could find out what was happening with Max and did he want to come to Holland.

'I wouldn't bother worrying about it,' he had said. 'I think we all know the answer.'

As the lads pile into their seats, their fathers arrange themselves at a safe distance. Every dad has come, except Luke's who is still banned for reasons of embarrassment. Not a single mother of our team is coming, though.

'Isn't it strange,' I hear my wife saying to Fraser's mum

as they stand together on the pavement, ready to wave us off, 'neither of them has even asked me what I'll do with myself when they're gone.'

And the pair of them snigger.

It is a long way to Holland by coach. Next time, I tell myself when I realise we've been going two hours but are still only somewhere north of Canterbury, I'll fly. I try to catch up on a bit of sleep. But give up when I realise that Steve and Andrea are not only going to insist on playing the video of *Grease* on a continuous loop, but are determined to sing along to it. Steve takes the John Travolta part, while this morning, Andrea is Olivia Newton-John. At one point the two of them are in the aisle, jiving, telling each other that they are the one that they want, ooh, ooh, ooh, honey. The boys at the back cheer and stomp and call for an encore. Or at least they do the first time. By the third, they would happily settle for *Love Story*, *Bridget Jones's Diary*, *Notting Hill*, anything other than *Grease*.

We reach the ferry just after breakfast. It is overrun with junior football teams heading over to the continent. It must be Britain's biggest export at Easter time, small boys sailing off to play football in Europe, accompanied by fathers keen to start drinking beer from the moment the ferry shuts its doors. As their dads drink, everywhere I look there are boys in tracksuits shovelling cash into the fruit machines, or buying sweets in the shop, or hanging over the railings on the deck, forever surprised that when they gob into the wind, it ends up not on the top of the head of the bald bloke down below, but in their own faces.

In the queue for the cafeteria, the gangs of lads eye each other warily, scanning attire to see what kind of club they each belong to. It is here, in this fashion show, that Doug's money-saving instincts come under forensic scrutiny. While other clubs are decked out in smart track-suits with the name of the club embroidered on the back and in many cases the boy's initials on the sleeve or chest, Doug has bought a job lot of cheap red nylon wind-cheaters to serve as our tour jackets and has spent much of the evening before we leave ironing the club's name on to the back of each one. Some of his letters are less firmly ironed into place than others. Paul, for instance, is standing in line representing ' ort i g h'. Which looks like how the Sun would report Wayne Rooney's latest four-letter outburst.

After we dock, it takes us more than five hours to drive to our destination. It would have been less than that, had Doug not insisted we stop at a tobacco warehouse just inside the France-Belgium border. Here the car park is packed with coaches from Wolverhampton and Hereford, Walsall and Haywards Heath. All of them are full of youthful footballers. Many of them have union flags in the back windows reading things like 'Hoylake Hurricanes on tour. Shag your women and drink your beer.' Barry and I agree that we can only admire their ambition, given that the team in question appears to be the under-thirteens.

We remain here for half an hour to allow the coach drivers to stock up on booze and baccy, filling up all avail-able boot space with their purchases.

'That's why they give me such a good price,' Doug tells me as we wander round the warehouse. 'I've told them they can say it's a joint purchase by all of us if we get stopped by the customs.'

He is, as he speaks, loading case after case of cheap wine into a trolley.

'Doug,' I say, 'I thought you said that after your operation the doctors told you that you had to give up boozing.'

'They did.'

'Well, what's that then?'

'Yeah, boozing. But wine doesn't count, does it?'

The whole journey so far, Barney has been at the back
of the coach with his mates, playing balloon football with
a couple of inflated condoms. The lot of them wet themselves every time a johnny floats forward into the adult
sections of the coach. I have been up near the front, with
Barry and Hamish, waxing nostalgic about the times when
the kids were eight and innocent and didn't regard playing
condom football as the height of subversive behaviour.

Thus, when I am standing in the gents at the tobacco
warehouse and my son comes in and stands next to me,
I realise this is the furthest we have ever travelled together
without exchanging a word. Once, when he was about
five, we had driven across Slovakia, just the two of us,
while the rest of the family, with Ellie suffering chronic
car sickness, had taken the train. He had not stopped
talking on that journey, hour upon hour of nattering, as
if his world would come to an end if he wasn't filling
every minute with chat. On the bus I could hear him all
right, cackling and hooting and shouting at the back. But
he was not talking to me. I am no longer a central part
of his existence, the rock around which he revolves. When
he was born, my mum embroidered him a Victorian-style
sampler, which has hung ever since in the hall at home.

'Dear Little One,' the homily on it reads, 'I wish you
two things/To give you roots and to give you wings.'

Over the last few months, without me noticing, he has
developed the wingspan of an albatross. Right now, he is
flapping away off into the distance.

'Ah, long time no see,' I say as he stands beside me.
'You all right?'

'Yup,' he says.

There is a pause.

'Dad,' he says.

'Yeah.'

'Thanks.'

'For what?'

'All this. It's a laugh.'

And with that he turns, walks out and rejoins Rory,
Tim and the rest of them poring over the cigarette counter,
feeling the packets of two hundred Marlboro Lights. I
walk out with a skip, a skip which sustains me through
at least one more screening of *Grease*.

We arrive late afternoon at the club that is to host the
tournament. It is unlike anything I have experienced in
England. There are two full-sized floodlit pitches, half a
dozen five-a-side pitches, a grandstand and a clubhouse
that is wholly different from ours. For a start it is not in
the early stages of being demolished by death-watch beetle.
Plus there are two bars, a committee room, a television
room and a fully stocked shop selling club kit. This is a
small town, much smaller than where we come from, yet
it has big-time facilities for sport. There's a lesson there
somewhere.

We all follow Doug into the main bar. As he walks in,
he is greeted like Odysseus returning home after a twenty-
year voyage. Dozens of Dutch people surround him. They
shout his name, they slap him on the back, they high-
five his sons, they kiss his wife, somebody whisks a giggling
Andrea round in a whirl. And for a moment she thinks
she really must be Olivia Newton-John. In the midst of

the melee of hugging and handshaking, Doug introduces me to the Dutch club chairman.

'Mr Chairman,' he says, 'meet the chairman of Northmeadow Youth.'

'But, Marty, I thought you were the chairman,' says the man, his English sharp enough to register his disappointment.

'Not any more,' says Doug. 'I've retired. Meet the new boss.'

'Good, very good,' says the man, grabbing me by the elbow and leading me towards the bar. 'So tell me, do you drink like Marty? Otherwise you cannot be called chairman.'

In our part of the world, we simply don't have football clubs like this. Rugby and cricket clubs, yes. But not football. I don't know why, but our game just isn't the focus of the local community like this. We don't have clubs that run teams from under-six to over-sixty, that have facilities that would turn many a Premiership outfit green with envy, that have full-time bar staff who ask your name when you buy your first drink and remember it when you buy your second, third and fifth. Here, I doubt there would be a three-month battle over the purchase of a catering kettle. They'd just go out and buy one.

'So,' says the chairman. 'When did you win the election to be chairman?'

'Election?' I say. 'There wasn't an election. I just sort of found myself chairman really.'

'I see. You are lucky man.'

'Lucky man?' I say. 'Right. I never thought of it like that.'

The next morning, all the teams in the tournament line up for an opening ceremony, our boys all with their hair

temporarily stained in red stripes, sprayed by a can of dye
that Kal brought along from home. They have spent the
night in the homes of local families. Barney is sharing
with Fraser and John. It's nice enough, he says, but he is
disappointed with the quality of the packed lunch he has
been given.

'Look,' he says to me, opening up a roll which contains
nothing more than a thin smear of margarine and sugar.
'That's all I got.'

'What did you have last night?'

'Pasta. With sugar.'

Whatever the cuisine, our boys look happy and together
and up for this their venture into European football. Which
is more than can be said for their fathers, who, not for
the first time, are regretting a lack of tented accommodation at a football tournament. It is drizzling, non-stop,
so insistent we can only assume that it is coming in via
a direct pipeline from North Wales. The boys' dye jobs
are soon trickling down their faces. Over on the far side
of the pitch, the visiting German team's supporters shelter
in a sizeable marquee they have put up, complete with a
generator, powering a string of fairy lights in their team
colours, plus a fridge full of beers. Several of our parents
don't even have anoraks, labouring as they do under the
illusion that simply coming overseas is guarantee enough
of good weather.

'In Holland it rains all the time, that is well known
about this country,' says Franz's dad, Karl, who has brought
with him several snug-looking waterproof layers. But then
he is German.

In Holland, it turns out, it is not only wet, but they
play football in double year groups. So most of our boys
are a year younger than most of their opponents. From

the kick-off of their first game, the difference in scale is
noticeable. But our lads hold their own, taking their lead
from a ferocious sliding tackle by Paul in the second
minute of their first match, which sends his opponent
skidding across the wet turf, the two of them ending up
in a pile with the linesman and several supporters on the
touchline. It is a fair challenge, the referee doesn't give
anything, but the Dutch team are enraged. They surround
the referee, complaining and pointing. He ignores them
and simply awards a throw-in. A moment or two later,
Kal crashes with a clatter into a fifty-fifty challenge. His
opponent, I note, spotting his arrival, withdraws slightly,
allowing him to win possession easily. As Kal tanks away
with the ball, Doug's neighbour Steve, who has been
standing watching the game with increasing excitement,
yells out from the touchline:

'That's it, lads. They don't like it up them. Get in there.
Get stuck in.'

Karl, standing beside me, sighs.

'For God's sake,' he says. 'That is so typically English.
That is what English football is all about – get stuck in,
get stuck in, get stuck in. No wonder you never win
anything.'

He has a point. But then soon everyone is conforming
to footballing type. The Dutch teams pass in neat, quick,
at times mesmerising triangles. But they can't seem to
convert that into goals and it is not long into the day
before they are arguing among themselves, shrugging in
exasperation, shouting at their coach, moaning about
tactics, making a fuss when they are substituted. Our
English lads are all sleeves-rolled-up determination, grit
in the tackle, lung-busting in their effort, but with a tactical
overview that does not consist of much more than chuck

it in the mixer and see what happens. As for the Germans, well, they do have the most efficient warm-up routine I have ever seen. It consists of a lot of clapping and shouting in unison which makes them sound, as they prepare for a game, like a bunch of US marines.

But the biggest cliché of all becomes apparent as the day wears on. It is increasingly obvious that the locals do not want the Germans to win. They'd be quite happy if we did, wouldn't worry if the Belgians did, would be thrilled if another Dutch side did; anyone as long as it's not the Germans. The Dutch simply hate the Germans. Every game they play, the supporters of all the other teams shout for their opponents and boo the Germans' every touch, hissing at them as if they were pantomime villains.

'Bloody Dutch,' says Karl as the boos echo round the ground. In a show of solidarity, he joins the German supporters for one game, chatting amiably with them over on the far touchline in front of their marquee. He returns at the final whistle, chuckling to himself.

'I have a German joke about the Dutch,' he tells us.

And we all look forward to that.

'Why is it that all Dutch children have big ears?'

'I don't know,' we all say. 'Why is it that Dutch children have big ears?'

'Well,' says Karl, barely able to contain his glee, 'it is because when they are young their parents take them to the German border and hold them up by the ears and say: "Look over there, that is where the world champions of football come from." And their ears, you see, they stretch and become big.'

He laughs heartily while we stand there stony-faced, waiting maybe for a punchline.

'It is a good joke, no?' he says.

'Well,' says Hamish. 'Perhaps it loses something in the translation.'

'Unlike this,' adds Steve. And he starts singing: 'Ten German bombers . . .'

We manage to shut him up after the first chorus.

It is a tough first day of competition, at times a lesson in football. We draw one game and lose two, both of them narrowly and unluckily, both of them after matching the opponents everywhere but in front of goal. With Lee only half fit and seemingly cowed by fear of another injury, we live up to the old dictum: if you don't take your chances, you don't win matches. Kal, though, is magnificent, back to his authoritative best.

After both defeats, the lads are convinced they should have won.

'If we had put that one away . . .' they tell each other as they queue up at the food stall for chips and mayonnaise. But they didn't. So they lost. Still, we have three more games tomorrow. Including one against the Germans.

At the end of the day's play, we all make our way to the bar, the boys to wait for their host families to pick them up, we fathers to wait for Doug. He is sitting in the middle of a group of appreciative locals, holding forth about the last time the Dutch came over to England. Until he completes his anecdote, until he has told everyone several times about how his wife had to extract one of the Dutch lads from the middle of the pitch at the end of the disco evening where he was improving international relations with a local girl, we can't go back to our hotel. I buy a round of beers at the bar, to keep us going while we wait and find myself standing next to Steve.

'I'm telling you, them lads of yourn done brilliant,' he says. 'Honestly, they made me proud to be British. 'Specially that big Asian lad you got in midfield. Gor', he ent half bloody hard innee.'

It was a long, long night of bars and restaurants and bars and coffee shops and bars. From what I can remember, I was in the Irish pub in town playing spoof with Hamish, Richard and several of our new Dutch best friends, with the losers paying for the rounds of whisky when Doug appeared and insisted we all go over to the clubhouse, where there was a disco for the lads in full swing. When we arrived, on the stage next to the bar, a Tina Turner lookalike drag act was stamping around, his spangly skirt riding so far up his legs those near the front were confronted with growing evidence that he was still very much a pre-op. Watching on were Doug's Dutch fan club. They greeted his arrival as if he were a brother emerging from a ten-year stretch in solitary.

'So,' I said to one of the fathers, when the love-in had temporarily abated, 'where are the lads?'

They were in an upstairs bar. Half a dozen of our lads, plus Doug's sons, were crowded round two local girls. Doug's sons were taking pictures of the girls with their mobiles and giggling at the results, the modern language of seduction. There was no adult up there, so I did no more than catch Barney's eye, nod and quickly disappear back downstairs. Just in time to catch the final mangling of 'Simply the Best', which featured a couple of the locals, Doug, Steve and Andrea, cavorting around on stage with an excitement that could hardly have been matched were it the real Tina Turner up there rather than some burly mechanic moonlighting in a padded bra and fright wig. And, I noticed on closer inspection, a sizeable moustache.

★   ★   ★

The next morning, I ask Barney how his evening went.

'It was OK. So how come you didn't stop for long?'

'Didn't want to cramp your style,' I say.

'There wasn't any style to cramp,' he says. 'There were only two girls there and Doug's sons moved in on them.'

'Yeah, I saw.'

'They were well impressed when they told them their dad was the chairman.'

'Well, your dad's the bloody chairman, why didn't you get in there?'

'Oh yeah,' he says. 'Forgot about that.'

The rain has not relented, and I change out of my clothes into tracksuit and football boots, leaving my stuff in the changing rooms. I head over to the pitches where the boys are waiting, edgy, nervy, excited for their encounter with the Germans. As I walk over, I realise that Steve has gathered them round and is giving them a pep talk.

'They're Krauts, boys,' he is saying. 'There's history here, lads. That's what you're playing for. Remember their grand-dads tried to kill your granddads.'

'They didn't try to kill my granddad,' says Franz. 'He is German.'

I attempt to introduce a slightly more rational note to proceedings, but Steve is having none of it. He has now embarked on a patriotic stream of consciousness.

'Get in there, boys,' he says. 'All for one and one for all. Battle of Britain, Dunkirk, Winston Churchill and all that. This is the big one.'

Maybe there is history here. Maybe it's a genetic thing. Maybe Steve has missed his vocation and should be in the England dressing room. Whatever the cause, the game is only half an hour long, but it is the most feisty perform-ance the lads have ever played. The Germans are better than them, more accomplished, more skilful, more organised. But the spirit of the English is a sight to behold. They work for each other, they try for each other, they will not be turned over.

Then, with not long to go and the Germans leading by the only goal, Luke launches himself at an opponent just in front of where most of our supporters are standing. He wins the ball, but the German lad doesn't like it, and, as he gets up, stamps on Luke's outstretched leg, yelling abuse as he does so. Barney, following up and closest to the incident, is furious at the attack. He pushes the German culprit over, bundling him to the ground. At that, several Germans take offence. But Barney does not back down. Chest out, chin forward, he barges into a couple of them as they confront him. A melee ensues. Kal and Paul pile in on Barney's behalf. Tim grabs one of their players by the throat. Luke, meanwhile, remains down on the ground, not injured, just keeping out of the way. The referee and the linesman quickly move in to break things up, and, amid much shouting and finger-pointing and threats of recrimination, with Steve looking as if he might run from the touchline to join in until he is held back by Karl, the ref shows the German lad the red card.

'Bloody right too,' Steve shouts.

The moral high ground is not held for long. As the German lad walks off, the ref turns to Barney and shows him the card.

'This is fair,' says Karl.

I have been coaching for six years now, constantly preaching a gospel of fair play and non-retaliation. And the first player to be sent off playing for our team is my own son. Before he leaves the pitch, Barney trots over to the German boy, who is heading off in the opposite direction and for a moment I think, Oh no, don't chin him. But he doesn't. He offers his hand to the boy, who shakes it and nods, their mutual respect acknowledged. All our supporters applaud Barney off, Steve in particular, slapping him on the back and saying:

'Well done, son, you wasn't standing for no Kraut shite. You stood up for yourself. You're a proper Englishman now, boy.'

Barney isn't listening. He walks over to the bench where we have piled all our stuff, moves aside a couple of tops now increasingly denuded of their lettering, sits down, puts his face in his hands and sobs. I go over to comfort him and he rests his head on my shoulder.

'Sorry,' he says, blubbing hard now. 'Shit, sorry.'

'Hey, come on,' I say as I stroke his hair like he's five again and just fallen off his bike. And I realise as I do so, that, for all the bravado, for all the Lynx, for all the testosterone, for all the hair sprouting in unruly fashion above his top lip, this is still a boy. It is, I think as he gradually recovers his poise, a moment I want to last for ever.

The Germans beat us and go on to win the tournament. At the presentation ceremony, their captain goes up to receive the trophy in almost complete silence, just about the only applause coming from Barney, Tim and a couple of our team. Steve stands alongside me shaking his head. When I go to change out of my boots, I find that someone has nicked my shoes. So I have to face a nine-hour coach journey, ninety-minute ferry crossing and numerous stops for rubbish motorway food and insipid motorway coffee, wearing muddy football boots. We are returning with a record of three defeats, two draws and only one victory, secured over the other English team in the tournament.

It takes us three-quarters of an hour to extract Doug from the well-wishers and back-slappers in the bar. Steve and Andrea have still not got *Grease* out of their system. And somebody has relieved me of my favourite shoes. But I am not remotely despondent. I can't quite put my finger on why that is until we arrive back home at three in the morning. As Barney and I are getting our bags out of the coach, moving cases of booze and boxes of fags to find them, I find myself standing alongside Steve.

'Well done, mate, your lads were great. And I tell you what, you look me in the eye and tell me you weren't secretly well proud of this old boy here when he smacked that Kraut. Go on, tell me you wasn't.'

'Not at all,' I say, aware that Barney is on my shoulder. 'Terrible indiscipline. Maybe cost us the game.'

But actually, Steve is right. Inside I am smiling.

24

The kettle

The committee meeting has now entered its third hour and the landlord has just called last orders. I had intended to raise several issues about the condition of the top pitch, FA coaching courses and who we are going to get to manage the under-eights next season now that the bloke we had originally earmarked for the position has resigned due to 'unexpected family commitments' (i.e. a sudden rush of sanity to the brain). But instead we have spent the last two and a bit hours discussing the condition of the tea bar. Ian believes the break-in offers us the chance to rebuild it as a fully functioning profit centre for the club. Malcolm is more concerned about how soon we can buy a replacement catering kettle. The insurance policy insists on a hundred-quid excess, so it scarcely seems worthwhile claiming, given that the kettle was the only thing to suffer in the intrusion. And Ian is adamant that – despite the fact the bank state-ment suggests we have twelve grand in our coffers – we cannot afford to waste money on non-essential frills. After an hour of discussion, I propose that I will buy a new kettle myself. Ian is not happy with this idea.

'This sets a very bad precedent. I am against the concept of committee members having to cover shortfall caused by organisational frailties,' he says.

'Are you referring to me?' says Malcolm.

I suggest we take a vote on it and Mike agrees. Ian, however, points out that a vote would not be constitutionally binding.

'We are not quorate,' he says.

He's right. There are only five people in attendance. Fifteen other members of the committee have sent me their apologies for absence, wisely discovering that they suddenly have a life to be getting on with on a Tuesday evening.

'Yes, and whose fault is it that we are not quorate?' says Malcolm.

'I take it you are suggesting it is mine,' says Ian. 'I am merely ensuring committee procedures are followed in line with the constitution.'

And so it goes on. Mentally I drift off, the only debate engaging my mind at this moment is the one about who should play where in Sunday's final.

'What's your opinion?' somebody asks, interrupting my flow just after I've nailed down the left side of midfield.

'Er, I think we should get a pint in before the pub shuts,' I say.

'I second that,' says Mike.

As we stand there at the bar, I point out to Mike that, as far as I can remember, we have not accomplished a single thing in the past year of committee meetings except scare away from attending at least half a dozen age-group managers who would prefer to spend their time coaching their teams rather than fight for power like bald men scrapping over a comb.

'Any chance', I say to him, 'that you might engineer a coup and have me removed from office?'

'No way, Mr Chairman,' he says. 'To stop the whole thing falling apart through infighting, we've got to have someone in the middle there who really, really doesn't care.'

25

The final

'Which would you rather,' says Barney as we head up to the clubhouse on the day of the final. 'That we won the cup and got relegated, or stayed up and lost today?'

'Course, you could do both: you could win the cup and stay up,' says Hugo, now our self-appointed chief cheerleader.

'Or we could do neither: lose the final and get relegated,' I say.

'God,' the two of them chorus, 'you are so pessimistic.'

Today, though it lurks in the background, malevolent and unyielding, relegation is not the issue. Today is the County Cup final. Today is the big one. It is the biggest game any of our players have ever played in. It is certainly the biggest game this particular manager has ever been involved in. There will be a crowd, there will be a matchday programme with the boys' names in it, there will be a fully functioning tea bar, complete with hot beverages. There will even be sausage and chips for the players afterwards. It really is that big.

Not that I am getting too excited. I have spent the

past few days trying to elicit advice about how to prepare in cup-final week from those who know about these things. And the consensus seems to be: don't get too excited. I interview Martin Buchan, the former Manchester United captain, for a piece about football in the seventies and he tells me overexcitement is the enemy of teams in cup finals. Beware of it, he cautions. He explains that before the 1976 FA Cup final too many of his team-mates had been distracted by the flim and flam and were mentally exhausted come kick-off. They had, he says, been temporarily blinded by the pound signs flashing up in front of their eyes, the chance to cash in on razor-blade adverts and commercial endorsements for frozen food. I remember it clearly. I was at that game, in my jumbo flares and stack-heeled boots, standing high on the Wembley terraces watching Gordon Hill and Steve Coppell toil round in pursuit of Southampton's players as if they had a hundredweight of sand in their boots.

Graham Taylor says much the same thing. He tells me there will be no need to gee the lads up, they will be more than aware of the significance of the event without me having to stick a verbal rocket up their backsides. In fact, he tells me it is more likely I will need to relax them, calm them down. Every single one of them will be alive with nervous energy. I ring Eric Harrison for advice about maybe a little training drill to adopt in the last session before the big game and he tells me that it is too late for that sort of thing.

'The work's done now,' he says. 'Just play a gentle bit of five-a-side. Make sure no one gets injured.'

The work's done? Oh bugger.

In fact it is Barry who comes up with the most pertinent bit of cup-final week thinking.

'They're going to remember this for the rest of their lives,' he says as we pack away the bibs and balls after that last training session. 'So we'd better make sure all the subs get a game. We don't want them remembering being sat on the bench for the rest of their lives.'

Barry, whose kindness to the boys remains unsurpassed, has also come up with a masterstroke. He tells everyone at training there will be a surprise in store on the big day and instructs us all to meet up at the clubhouse, even those who normally make their way directly to a game. As we all gather there, round the corner comes a swish new coach, significantly smarter than the ones Doug had booked for the trip to Holland. Aboard it is Barry. As the door opens he steps out on to the pavement to a spontaneous round of applause. It gets better: on each of the sixteen seats at the back of the bus is a smart, new tracksuit, with our name embroidered on the back and each boy's squad number on the sleeve. Proper kit at last.

'Thought we'd travel there in style,' says Barry.

Everyone – players, parents, step-parents, same-sex life partners, young female supporters with the name of their favourite scribbled in marker pen across their burgeoning embonpoint – piles aboard for the half-hour trip to the stadium. Even Luke's dad is here.

'No longer an embarrassment?' I say.

'I've been told I'm in the clear,' he says. 'As long as I don't say anything at all, all day.'

'That's you in trouble already, then,' I say.

I had been working on my pre-match speech for some time, thinking about it when I should be working, constructing it clause by clause when I should be discussing A-level choices with my daughter, rehearsing it at five in the morning when I can't sleep. After we have posed for endless team photos taken by mums and grans and young girls (Tim must be the wallpaper on the mobiles of half the fourteen-year-old females in town), the boys and I take possession of our changing rooms. We can hear the opposition next door, the clack of studs on the tiled floor, the giggles, the excitement.

For maybe the first time in their existence as a team, as I start to speak the boys are silent, attentive. Luke is not preparing a pratfall, Gio does not set Tim off giggling with a sly glance, Barney is simply staring at his feet. Graham Taylor is right: there is no geeing up needed here.

Instead, borrowing heavily from the Al Pacino character in the American football movie *Any Given Sunday*, I tell them that trophies are won by those who give the extra inch. By that stretch to clear a corner, by that lunge that connects with a cross rather than just misses, by the player that runs back to cover that extra bit quicker than normal, that's how they will win. Thankfully, none of them has seen the film.

'And I have no doubt you will win it,' I say. 'I have known you all now for six years. I have been privileged to be associated with people like you. I know you. I know you can do it. So let's go . . .'

When I finish, Tim shouts: 'Cooomon lads', and they all join in an incoherent shout, a chance to let out some of that tension. I lead them out of the changing room, into the corridor, as the *Match of the Day* theme plays over the stadium public address system, out into the big time.

What my speech doesn't contain is much analysis of the opposition. There is little need: Castleton have won their league already, for the fourth season on the trot.

When it comes to dominance of boys' football round our way, they make Chelsea look amateurs. They appear organised, professional, sorted even, as they set themselves for the kick-off. But then my boys look good, too. As I stand next to Barry at the edge of our technical area, I look round at Rory, and Paul and Kal and Ryan and Tim and think, They'll do for me; I wouldn't swap this bunch for the world. In the middle of the back four is my own son, about to play football at a level his father never came close to attaining. And the best thing of all is, he doesn't look out of place.

If life had the resolution of a movie, if this had been a book about a little league baseball team from the wrong side of the tracks playing their way from small-town obscurity to the national pennant play-off, then you would know the outcome of the game. We would win the cup, of course we would. Not just simply win it, either. But win it after facing a last-minute drama in which Rory is injured while giving away a penalty. While I am crouching over him as he lies in pain, just as Barry shakes his head to indicate the poor lad can't go on, Barney taps me on the shoulder and points up to the stand. And there I see Max, sitting at a slight distance from our supporters, a late arrival who has made his way to the game on his own, to see how his mates get on. He is sitting just along from Jeff and JJ, who have turned up to shout for the opposition. I beckon him down on to the pitch. He points at his chest and mouths the words, 'What? Me?' He pulls on Rory's shirt and, after he has made a crucial, blinding, brilliant save to win it for us, I go over to him and say: 'Now will you believe me that you are a goalkeeper?' Then the camera pans upwards and away, with me and

Max a still, steady centre in a whirligig of celebration and high-fiving.

But the truth is, Max is nowhere in sight, he has slipped quietly and without fuss off our collective radar. He is probably, even as Rory dives and scrambles in his stead, lying at home, in bed, asleep and oblivious to our endeavours. And life is not Hollywood and sport does not run to some easy script of redemption and pat self-discovery. Which is a roundabout way of saying, yeah, sure, we lose the game.

It is immediately obvious from the moment it begins why it is Castleton win everything in their path: the excellence of their passing and movement is sustained. When they take the lead in the first half, I think, Oh well, it's good to have got this far. But my lads counter their opponents' superior technique with the most astonishing display of spirit, a togetherness forged, I think, during that bundle against the Germans. So hard do they graft for each other, so fearsomely do they tackle, so grimly determined are they in every facet of their work, they actually do shed blood for the cause. Paul is sent from the fray by the referee with a big gash on his knee, the blood gushing down his socks. Barry cleans him up and as he does so his father, the distinguished lawyer, leans over the barrier running round the pitch.

'Paul, what's the matter with you?' he says. 'It can't hurt that much, now get out there.'

I feel redundant on the touchline. My input is little more than to ensure the subs all have a chance (even Lee, stalked all season by injury after injury, gets a run-out, a ten-minute flourish to show us what might have been).

And their effort gains some reward. First Ryan equalises, then Faisal puts us in the lead. Oh yes, for ten minutes in the County Cup final we are in the lead. It doesn't last. Castleton get one back and then, in the first period of extra time, score a winner of such quality it is hard not to stand back and admire it. Which is roughly what Barney and the rest of the defence do.

The Hollywood ending suggests that it can only be through victory that you can learn life lessons. I watch the boys after the game and realise this is hokum. At the final whistle, you can see in their opponents' eyes, used as they are to trouncing everyone they meet, a real respect as they shake hands and commiserate. Their manager tells our boys they are the best team his lads have ever faced. I smile at that. Then the lads trot over as a group to where their family and friends are gathered in the stadium's main stand. This is where Hamish has been growling throughout the game. This is where Hugo has been maintaining an unending barrage of chants, adapting Premiership favourites for each player, then going off on a few bizarre tangents including one for Rory based on the Christmas carol 'God Rest Ye Merry, Gentlemen.' Not really going to catch on at Millwall that one.

Once they are here, the boys all hug their mums and dads and stepdads and same-sex life partners. Even Luke appears to have forgiven his father and is enjoying a moment of mutual, unembarrassed affection. As the pictures are taken and the videos completed, I look into faces and realise this: they have done their best and that in itself is an achievement. They have pitched themselves at the top and not been embarrassed. There are no tears of self-pity, no whingeing about referees or an unlucky bounce of the ball. They can face defeat with equanimity because they have given everything. And that is what counts. That is sport's great lesson.

As for me, I wouldn't swap what I have learned coaching these boys for every trophy in Ryan Giggs's cabinet. With this lot, we may not have put a single cup up on the shelves of the cupboard next to the tea bar, but we have achieved something much more valuable. Win nothing with kids? As I make my way off the pitch after the cup final, I feel like I have won everything.

Postscript

So why, then, if winning doesn't matter, am I now standing on the touchline of our relegation rivals' pitch picking up the several pieces of my mobile phone that I have just flung to the ground in disgust after we concede another goal to go 3-0 down in the game we have to win to avoid the drop? If defeat has its own special dignity, how come I am in such a fury at the prospect of its imminent arrival? If losing is such a good thing, how come I feel sick to my stomach?

Well, it's easy to say it. Winning doesn't matter. There, said it. But today defeat has much wider repercussions. It will mean we are relegated. It will mean we have just endured a season-long failure. It will signal that despite the cameo of the cup final, over an entire nine-month term we are not good enough to live in the best company. And that is a thought that hurts sufficiently to jeopardise the safety of my phone.

When I first started to coach this team, I did almost everything wrong. I shouted too much, I projected my anxieties from the touchline, I got stressed, I got moany.

None of it worked. I have had six years to learn on the job, which is a lot longer than most football managers are gifted. Frankly, looking back on how I first was as a manager, if I'd been the chairman then I would have sacked myself.

But the thing I have learned most of all is this: nobody ever got better through being blamed. Even the cockiest kid, the one who your instincts shout at you to belittle and bring down a peg or two, thrives on praise. Actually, he probably needs it more than the centred, sensible lad alongside him.

So at this precise moment, as the referee blows his whistle for half-time and my phone lies in pieces around my feet, the very last thing I should do is apportion blame. Nobody, not one of them, has meant to fail like this. They didn't turn up here this morning hoping to be in this position. I really need to suppress every instinct to shout, 'What the bloody hell was that?', and come up with some-thing inspirational. But the only half-time speech that springs to mind as the boys tramp wearily in my direc-tion, their heads down and their gaze on the ground, is one of Brian Clough's. He gave it once when Nottingham Forest were losing 2-0 at the end of the first forty-five minutes, and the players made their way into the dressing room in anticipation of a humungous bollocking. The manager, though, wasn't even there. They waited for him to arrive, but he didn't. So they started to sort things out among themselves. Soon, they heard the referee knock on the door, indicating half-time was over. They were just about to head back on to the pitch, when Clough finally appeared, stuck his head round the door and said: 'Sorry lads, all my fault. Picked the wrong team.'

It is a good line. But, as I look at Tim and Paul and

Rory and Ryan and Kal and Faisal and Barney, especially Barney, eyes filled with misery, the urge to kick them when they are down immediately deserts me. They look so unhappy, there is no point telling them they have just played the worst, most nerve-racked, incompetent half of football they have played all season. Judging by the looks on their faces, and the tears flowing unchecked down Tim's cheeks, they know it.

'All right, lads,' I say. 'Forget what happened there. That's over. Fact is, you've got forty minutes left. Either that can be the last forty minutes' football you will ever play in the A League. Or you can go out there and do something about it. It's up to you. Only you can do it now. Barry and I can't help you. It would be great if we could put Bazz on the pitch, but I think the opposition would notice. Only you can do it. Only you can rescue what we've worked for. It's down to you, lads. So go out there and do it.'

I don't expect them to. I turn to Barry and say: 'Well, they dug the hole.' My wife, who is standing away off behind one of the goals, looks at me and shakes her head sadly.

But on the touchline, Hamish isn't defeated. He growls his war cry, and a couple of the other parents join in. So do I. And so does Barry. And then my wife. Suddenly, against any prevailing logic, I can feel something in the air.

It takes another twenty minutes for the plot to reach its climax, but in the end, it all gets a bit David Pleat out there. All I need is a pair of grey slip-ons and an ill-fitting suit and my impression of the loopy Luton manager, celebrating his side's improbable escape from relegation at

Maine Road back in the eighties, would be complete. Thankfully there is nobody with a video camera recording my performance. I really would not like to watch it rewound.

It goes roughly like this. There are only twenty minutes of our A League existence remaining when Lee scores the first, throwing off a season-long injury curse to dance through their defence. In response, there is a lot of fist-pumping from me and scarcely intelligible shouting of a 'we can do this, cooomon, lads' variety. After Kal gets his foot to the ball following the goalie dropping it, there is a dash along the touchline featuring a Mike Channon windmill arm action which brings me into contact with the big tall Welshman with the grumbly baritone who is supporting the opposition. I apologise and the Welshman says, 'No worries, mate, I can see you can't help making a prat of yourself.'

Prat, though, barely covers what happens two minutes later when from a corner the ball drops to Fraser on the edge of the area and he smacks home the equaliser. At this point I leap into Hamish's arms and kiss him on each cheek. By now every single one of our parental supporters is shouting in a mix of disbelief and hope. I run behind them demanding more from them, and they all roar, all of them, mums, dads, stepdads, same-sex life partners, the lot. Behind the goal, my wife and Barry are hugging each other in a way that might, in other circumstances, have provoked suspicion. Over the other side of the pitch, Karl, acting as our linesman, later reports that the opposition manager is getting ever more furious at our antics: 'Bloody hell, they're all adults, you'd think they'd know better.'

We don't. When Paul scrambles in the fourth I go completely loopy, running on to the pitch and performing some sort of José Mourinho business with my arms. I notice that Hamish, perhaps fearing further advances, keeps his distance. Luke, off the pitch to have a wound attended to, runs past me and does a perfect slide tackle on the scorer who is running towards us, arms outstretched. As they both lie on the ground hugging, the rest of the team pile on top in an impromptu scrum. When they finally separate at the referee's insistence, Paul is bleeding heavily from a nose wound. Even his father agrees it might not be a bad idea if he comes off for medical attention. By now, our opponents are completely finished. They look shell-shocked at the force of nature that has overtaken them. I don't blame them. I don't know where it has come from. It wasn't from me, that's for sure. Maybe someone on the touchline has prayed for a miracle. Because that is what is happening.

But it isn't over. With only a minute or so to go, I shout at everyone to fall back to defend, protect our lead. They aren't listening. They can't resist the urge to charge forward: momentum pulling them like gravity towards their opponents' goal. Gio, a wise head in the madness, holds the ball by the corner flag, whiling away the seconds. He wins a corner. Kal, despite instructions to play it short, flights it into the box. They clear it, but don't have the legs to dash after it. The ball falls to Tim, who strides forward, beats two limp tackles from utterly finished opponents and hits the fifth. Forty minutes earlier the big lad was in tears. Now, as the final whistle goes, he simply cannot stop smiling.

So we get our victory in the one that really matters, after all. We are still in the A League. Though I don't suppose any of us are better people for it and the world has not been put to rights (for a start, at the time of writing the kettle issue has still to be resolved). As Barney and I walk back to the car after the celebrations have died down, I put my arm round his shoulder. He does the same to me. I realise as we walk that he is now taller than I am.

'Barns,' I say.

'Yeah?' he says.

'Thanks.'

'What for?'

'For all this. It's been a laugh.'

And we make our way to the car, discussing line-ups and formations for next season.